Natural Lifestyle Cooking

A Step Beyond Cooking,
Designed To Add Joy
And Years To Your Life.

By Mark and Ernestine Finley

INDEX

ISBN 0-9625343-1-5

Before We Start Cooking, Let's Uncover...

Three Vegetarian Myths

||T|| he scientific evidence is in, and it's conclusive. A balanced vegetarian diet is better for you than one which includes meat, especially red meat. A host of comparative studies have demonstrated that fact. For example, middle-aged males who regularly eat meat have been found to suffer from fatal coronary heart disease three times more than vegetarian males of the same age.

Author John Robbins concluded, "We can overwhelmingly reduce our potential for heart disease by eating a diet that supports the health of our cardiovascular system." A meat-based diet has also been linked to various types of cancer. One study found that the consumption of animal protein in animal fat was directly proportional to breast and colon cancer rates. That is, the more meat eating, the higher the risk of contracting those cancers.

The Major Killers Are Largely Preventable

Fifty years ago, most medical researchers believed that the major killers of our time — heart disease, stroke and cancer — were largely the unavoidable consequences of the aging process. Today, there is a sense that these diseases are not inevitable. Medical researchers today recognize that these diseases are largely preventable.

In his book, *The Vegetarian Handbook*, Roger Doyle shares some interesting insights from Europe on the effect of diet in the Scandinavian countries during World War I and World War II. "During World War I, when the allied blockade cut off most imports into Denmark, the Danes were faced with an alarming food shortage. For years they had depended on foreign sources for more than half their bread, grains and for much of their animal foods. In this extreme situation, the Danish Government in 1917 turned to Dr. Mikkel Hindehede of the Laboratory For Nutrition Research in Copenhagen. His advice, 'Stretch available grain supplies by slaughtering the livestock and using the grain as human food.' And so for more than a year, most Danes became virtual vegetarians with their principle fare being barley, porridge, potatoes, green vegetables, milk and a limited amount of butter. Their staple bread was whole grain rye with wheat bran added, a high fiber food." During this one-year period, remarkably most Danes lost weight — possibly because they didn't find their new diet attractive. However, the general improvement of their health was amazing. As Roger Doyle reports, " _____

_____ . "

Norway had a similar experience under Nazi occupation in World War II. They, of course, used less meat, milk, cheese, cream, eggs, fruit and sugar, but ate more fish, skim milk, potatoes, and vegetables. They had fewer calories, which meant they were consuming less fat, less sugar, and less cholesterol. Their consumption of fiber went way up.

During the Second World War, deaths from _____ , _____ and

_____ . Throughout Scandinavia and the northern European countries, cardiovascular disease went dramatically down during this war. Studies in cultures around the world indicate a high-fat diet produces heart disease and that a diet that is low in fiber, and high in sugar, fat and cholesterol, contributes to both cancer and heart disease.

Dr. Dennis Burkett and Hugh Trowell, British physicians, demonstrated conclusively that rural Ugandans who hardly ever get colon cancer, eat considerable amounts of fiber. Americans and Europeans who are much more apt to suffer from the disease, generally get far less fiber (Roger Doyle, *The Vegetarian Handbook*, pages 4, 5).

Other dietary studies, have linked other animal consumption with high cholesterol, high blood pressure, angina pectoris, osteoporosis, kidney stones, urinary stones, and rheumatoid arthritis—not a crowd we would want to associate with. But here is the good news! Several studies have demonstrated that a vegetarian diet often reverses many of the health problems that arise from eating meat. **We can actually help cure chronic health problems by our diet.**

Now all this is very hard evidence to argue against, but that doesn't mean it sinks in for those of us who need to hear it most. Many people, in fact, go on with high-risk dietary habits, all the while congratulating themselves on their healthy red-blooded lifestyle. The facts about which foods are best and which foods aren't are often obscured by various popular myths. In this first portion of the Natural Lifestyle nutrition series, we're going to expose three of the vegetarian myths that seem to influence us the most.

THE FIRST MYTH IS THIS: A VEGETARIAN DIET IS ONE FOR THE FRINGES OF SOCIETY, NOT THE MAINSTREAM

The popular notion is that since most people eat meat, and meat is the acceptable diet of the majority, a vegetarian diet is reserved for some academics, scholars, and over-zealous health conscious people, or some faddish young people, as well as some wild-eyed religious fanatics.

Let's look at the facts:

1. _____ or _____% are actively reducing their red meat consumption.

2. Meat consumption per capita in the United States is at its _____ since the early 1960s.

3. The number of vegetarians in the U.S. has more than _____

   to _____ .

4. Grocery shoppers interested in _____ are growing at the rate of

   _____ per week.

Vegetarianism is entering into the mainstream in North American culture. More and more restaurants are carrying a healthy fare section on their menus to accommodate the large number of growing vegetarians. Athletes, actors and actresses, public officials, educators, social scientists, doctors and nurses, factory workers, and a host of young people are adopting a vegetarian diet. Many grocery stores have vegetarian sections.

There are a growing number of meat analogs that are available today that are soya or gluten-based products produced by Worthington Foods, Sovex Natural Foods, Morning Star Farms, or Cedar Lake Foods. These meat analogs provide adequate protein without the harmful residual effects of meat. Many of them are readily available in grocery stores across the country.

President Clinton and the Meat Inspection Problem

The growing concern regarding the health problems associated with meat has even been discussed by the President of the United States in recent weeks. The July 7, 1996 edition of the Boston Sunday Globe contains an article by Reuters News which was printed in major newspapers around the world. In the article, President Clinton comments, "Parents should note that when a teenager borrows the car to get a fast-food hamburger, the hamburger should be the least of their worries." Clinton was referring to a January 1993 food poisoning outbreak in the Pacific Northwest that killed four children and made 500 people sick. The outbreak was traced to the virulent Ecoli 0157:H7 bacteria in undercooked hamburger served by a chain of fast-food restaurants.

The Clinton administration actually made a commitment to modernize the meat inspection system after this Pacific Northwest outbreak. Until now, government inspectors have been examining meat and poultry visually to certify that it's safe. This is the same way they have been inspecting meat for the last 90 years, since the meat inspection act was enacted in 1907.

According to Reuter's News Service, _____ and more than _____ die each year because of contaminated meat and poultry products. If sicknesses directly caused by contaminated products could be eliminated, in the United States we would save between $990 million and $3.7 billion a year. This, of course, has led President Clinton to this massive attempt in reorganizing the meat inspection system. The meat industry, while it welcomes the new rules, has consistently opposed these government testing standards because it says, "There can be _____ that disease-causing pathogens can be eliminated."

If we are going to spend close to $90 million a year attempting to overhaul the meat inspection system with very little assurance that these disease-causing pathogens can be eliminated, would it not be wiser to educate people toward a vegetarian diet? It appears that now is the time for a vegetarian diet to go into the mainstream. It is a myth to think that the vegetarian diet is just for a few off in the fringes. The evidence is in. A vegetarian diet is the healthiest.

VEGETARIAN MYTH #2: A VEGETARIAN DIET PROVIDES INADEQUATE PROTEIN

This myth has been perpetuated for years. Protein is America's nutritional "sacred cow" say Aileen Ludington, M.D. and Hans Diehl, DHSC, MPH, in their fascinating book, *Lifestyle Capsules*, page 105. They go on to say, "Cooks plan meals around it. The media exploit it. We worry about getting enough of it, yet the facts are that most people eat two or three times more protein than they need."

There are some major problems with an excessively high protein diet. This extra protein places _____ which may be one of the reasons for the high incidence of kidney disease in Western society. High-protein diets are also increasingly associated with osteoporosis. Most of the protein eaten by Westerners comes from animal sources and is loaded with excessive cholesterol and saturated fat, which contributes to atherosclerosis and narrowing and hardening of the arteries and the increase of plaque in the vital oxygen carrying arteries. This process accelerates_____ and _____ life, according to Drs. Ludington and Diehl. Many Americans get _____ from meats and dairy products.

Inadequate Research Leads to the Protein Myth

How did this protein myth get started? At the turn of the century, Carl Voit, a German research scientist studying coal miners in Bavaria, recommended the daily protein allowance of 100 grams. He observed that these coal miners were veritably healthy, had unusual amounts of endurance, and were physically fit. He then assumed that since they were eating a hundred grams of protein, that must be the norm. Shortly after that in 1904, Yale University's Russell Chippenden contended that 100 grams of protein was far too much and that 50 grams was enough.

Recent studies indicate that as few as 30 - 40 grams of protein a day may be better. The presently recommended dietary allowance, the RDA established by the Food and

Nutritional Board of the National Academy of Sciences, is _____ .

It's possible that advice about protein may have effected the outcome of the first World War. This intriguing possibility is raised by the extraordinary case of Dr. Max Rubner. In 1914, he was a man of great influence in German scientific circles. He was also a strong proponent of the idea that protein promotes vigor and physical efficiency. In the words of an authoritative nutritional text, "He probably did more than any other Army general to lose the war, for on his advice German agriculture was continued on the old policy of raising large herds of cattle and sheep. No additional pastures were plowed. His failure to realize that cereals can yield up to six times more dietary energy per acre than cattle contributed importantly to the defeats which followed in 1917" (Davidson Etal, *Human Nutrition and Dietetics*, Sixth Edition, Edinburgh, Churchill Livingston, 1975, page 69).

Overestimating protein needs may have led Dr. Rubner to develop an agricultural policy which caused Germany to have inadequate food supplies for their soldiers. This idea of over-protein continues as a common practice in our society today. Adele Davis in her best-selling booklet, *Eat Right To Keep Fit*, claimed that lack of protein was "the greatest hindrance to good health." She then went on to assume that 60 percent of affluent people in America get inadequate protein. Now this mistaken emphasis on high protein consumption has contributed to the myth that a vegetarian diet provides inadequate protein.

Medical researchers today are debunking that myth. Dr. Mervyn Hardinge stated, "With adequate amounts of fruits, nuts, grains and vegetables, it's impossible not to get the adequate protein the body needs." Harvard University's Fredrick Stare added, "It's highly unlikely that protein deficiency will ever result from a diet that is abundant in fruits, nuts, grains and vegetables."

Vegetarians who get the bulk of their calories from _____ , _____ ,

_____ and _____ , should have no problem in staying well above the safe

minimum protein level as estimated by the World Health Organization. _____

_____ . There may be a protein inadequacy if individuals drastically cut their calories as in some weight-reducing crash diets. Teenage girls who binge and purge or develop bulimia or anorexia may also develop protein deficiencies, but a balanced vegetarian diet is certainly safe.

A well-rounded vegetarian diet that freely uses fruits, nuts, grains, and vegetables, along with nuts and seeds, and some dairy products used sparingly, provides all of the protein the body needs. Years of research have consistently demonstrated that the amino acids that make up protein that the body does not produce are easily available from a random selection of vegetarian plant foods. Dietary patterns around the world consistently demonstrate this. The Caribbean countries with their black beans and rice, Mexico with corn tortillas and pinto beans, and the rice and soybeans relied upon by the Chinese all provide adequate protein. Foods that are low in fat, high in fiber, free of cholesterol and have plenty of protein provide adequate nutrition.

Hans Diehl and Aileen Ludington made the point clearly when they said, "It's time to bury the myth and catch up with the times. Increasing the amount of protein you eat to RDA levels is a good place to start. With protein as with much else in life, too much of a good thing is a bad thing." (See *Lifestyle Capsules*, Hans Diehl and Aileen Ludington, pages 105-107). Let's bury the myth that vegetarians don't get adequate protein as we move on to Myth Number Three.

VEGETARIAN MYTH #3: THE VEGETARIAN DIET DOES NOT PROVIDE ADEQUATE STRENGTH

Vegetarianism may be okay for bookworms or people who do nothing more strenuous than reading a book, but for really active people, red meat is essential.

No sports figure, it is often said, could survive on a mere vegetable protein. Is it possible for a vegetarian athlete really to compete successfully against meat-eaters? How could they build muscle? What about strength, endurance, and bulk?

There is no doubt that vegetarians can compete successfully against those who eat meat. Here are some examples. Mary Rose, a vegetarian, was a triple gold medal winner in the 1956 Olympic swimming events. The same year, another vegetarian, William Pickering, swam the English Channel in record time. Alexander Anderson, an Australian vegetarian, is a record-holder in weight lifting. Can you imagine that? Here's a sport that requires muscular strength.

Think about those Olympic athletes. Weight lifters, solid as steel, muscular giants, amazing physiques, and a vegetarian among them, at the top? With a world record? A number of professional football players have also been vegetarians. They claimed that they played better since becoming a vegetarian. Peter Burwash, another vegetarian, was the top ranked tennis player in both Canada in 1971 and in Hawaii in 1973.

A Vegetarian Triathalon Champion

Dave Scott would certainly disagree that it's necessary to eat meat to have adequate muscles and endurance. And Dave has quite a list of credentials to back him up. Dave Scott has been one of the regulars competing in the Iron Man Triathalon held on the coast of Hawaii. What does this triathalon entail. First, swimming 2.4 miles in the ocean, then biking 112 miles along the coast and finally running a full 26.2 mile marathon. All this in succession, on the same day. Just to finish the event is a remarkable accomplishment of strength and stamina. Did you get the full impact of this — swimming, biking, and a marathon! What a tax on the human body! What a fatiguing, absolutely nerve shattering day! Think of the endurance and the strength necessary. But Dave Scott has won the event six times. In 1986 he set the Iron Man record of 8 hours 28 minutes and 37 seconds. I don't think anyone could doubt that this one man is in the peak of physical condition. And he is thriving as an athlete on a vegetarian diet. Dave Scott made the choice that vegetarianism is something best for his body. He believes he competes better and is in better physical and mental shape than his meat-eating opponents. Dave Scott is not alone.

Another rising star in marathon is Cindy New of Montreal, Canada, who has trained on a vegetarian diet for some time. Recently Cindy said this: "Many world class runners are now turning toward vegetarianism."

Obviously, the idea that active people must have meat in their diets is simply fiction. Protein is protein. Nuts, grains, and vegetables have an abundant supply to meet all of our food needs. In fact, one dietary study demonstrated that it's almost impossible for vegetarians to become protein deficient if the right body weight is maintained.

These Vegetarians Run 100 to 200 Miles a Day

The most unusual vegetarian athletes in the world are the Tarahumara Indians. The Tarahumaras who live in the Sierra Madre Mountains of Northern New Mexico play a game called "Raripuri" in which competing teams of two or three players run almost continually for 100 to 200 miles kicking a wooden ball about the size of a small grapefruit up and down the rugged mountain paths. Even at night the contest goes on by torchlight with the players stopping briefly every 13 miles or so for a small amount of food and water. The Tarahumaras rarely eat eggs, dairy products or meat, and most of their calories come from corn and peas supplemented with potatoes, squash, pumpkin, chili peppers, citrus fruits and other fruits and vegetables. Their endurance is remarkable. They hardly stop during that 100 to 200 mile race. What an example of the adequacy of a vegetarian diet.

The Hunzas

A number of years ago, the founder of our It Is Written television program, Pastor George Vandeman, and our film crew traveled to the Himalayas at the invitation of the king of Hunza. The Hunzas came to international notoriety because they were one of the longest living civilizations in the world. They are largely vegetarians who subsist on the fruits, nuts, grains, and vegetables which they grow. They drink abundant amounts of fresh glacial water and breathe the Himalayan mountain air of Northern Pakistan. On one occasion when the king desired to have a new piano, it was shipped by plane to a town 50 miles away. Eight men walked the 50 miles that day, picked up the piano and walked back the same day with it. Their strength is absolutely incredible.

And they are vegetarians. Yes, it's a myth that vegetarianism is not for the mainstream. Certainly it's a myth that the vegetarian diet does not provide adequate protein. And it's a myth that the vegetarian diet does not provide adequate endurance.

A vegetarian diet _____ . In a vegetarian diet there is a

_____ . Vegetarian populations

are _____ . The vegetarian diet provides for a

_____ life. Vegetarians generally live _____ .

A vegetarian diet increases the _____ .

As soon as an animal dies, enzymes are released that begin the process of decay. As we've noted, to preserve meat is a major challenge. Pesticides and fertilizers used on the animal's food can be rapidly absorbed into the body and the residue is left in the meat. A

vegetarian diet _____ .

    Yes, a vegetarian diet will go a long way to bring your family health, happiness, and longevity. After all, when the Creator made this world He gave us an abundance of fruits, nuts, grains, and vegetables in the Garden of Eden. The one that made us and loves us with an everlasting love longs for us to be healthy. He provided Nature's Diet at the beginning to give us optimum health.

    This does not mean it is necessary to go home and throw all the meat out of your refrigerator. Gradual dietary changes are normally best. Establish a strategy in your mind and go home today deciding to put that strategy into practice. Commit yourself to living a positive, healthy lifestyle and watch the benefits that you will receive as you put these principles to practice in your life.

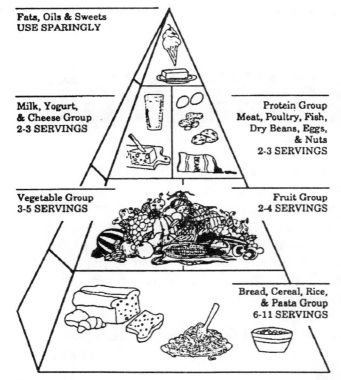

Fats, Oils & Sweets
USE SPARINGLY

Milk, Yogurt,
& Cheese Group
2-3 SERVINGS

Protein Group
Meat, Poultry, Fish,
Dry Beans, Eggs,
& Nuts
2-3 SERVINGS

Vegetable Group
3-5 SERVINGS

Fruit Group
2-4 SERVINGS

Bread, Cereal, Rice,
& Pasta Group
6-11 SERVINGS

ANSWER SHEET
Three Vegetarian Myths

Page 2: the death rate from non-infectious diseases fell by 34%; stroke, heart disease, other cardio-vascular diseases fell 21%
Page 3:
    1. 75 million, 40
    2. lowest level
    3. doubled, 15 million
    4. meatless selections; 20,000
Page 4: five million become ill; 4,000; no guarantee; added burdens on kidneys; aging, shortens, 50-85% of their calories
Page 5: 56 grams for average men and 44 grams for women; vegetables, grains, nuts, seeds; Lacto-ovo vegetarians who rely on dairy products have less of a problem
Page 8: increases health; decreased risk of disease; remarkably free of killer diseases; healthier and longer; longer; possibility our food is safe; increases the potential of world food supplies

Natural Lifestyle Cooking

Session 1

Homemade Breadmaking
Made Easy

Introduction

Situated on top of a cliff overlooking the emerald blue waters of the Mediterranean is an ancient Portuguese monastery. The view is breathtaking. The scenery is magnificent. But there is one problem. The only way to get to the top of the cliff is in an old wicker basket tied to a rope and hoisted up by an aged monk.

One day a guide and visitor were leaving the monastery. As they stepped into the basket and were lowered down by the monk, the rope swung out over the jagged rocks below. Nervously the tourist asked, "How often do they replace the rope?" "Don't worry," the guide replied in a reassuring tone, "every time one breaks, we replace it."

Just as in this story, thousands of people place themselves in an unpredictable situation regarding their health. They wait until their health snaps, like the rope, then frantically grasp onto the latest health fad. Broken health is not as easily replaced as a snapped rope! Health is not a matter of chance. It is a matter of obedience to nature's laws.

Let me commend you on the wise choice you have made by attending these natural foods cooking classes. During our seminar we shall present scientifically proven, common-sense, and widely accepted principles of nutrition. You will discover how to prepare healthy, delicious, and well-balanced meals that will bring enjoyment to the table and may add years to your life.

I. Nutrition and Your Health

While infectious diseases were the major killers in the western world one hundred years ago, a radical change has occurred in the 20th century. The leading killers now are the degenerative diseases such as heart disease, cancer, and arteriosclerosis. Although this may not seem like good news, it is. Degenerative diseases are generally associated with lifestyle choices — factors within your control.

A. _____ out of ten leading causes of death in America are diet related.

B. According to the Senate Select Committee on Human Needs, improved nutrition could cut the nation's health bill by _____ _____ .

C. During this century, the American diet has gone through an amazing transformation. Natural carbohydrates (fruits, vegetables, grains, and beans) which were the mainstay of the American diet, now play a

_____ role.

D. Fat and sugar consumption have risen to the point where they comprise at least _____ % of the American diet.

In this series of nutrition classes we shall assist you in:

1. increasing the natural foods in your diet.

2. reducing your overall fat consumption.

3. reducing your sugar consumption.

4. replacing flesh meats with vegetarian proteins.

5. preparing delicious, well-balanced, and natural food dishes.

6. Increasing the overall amount of fiber and whole grains in your diet.

Our first session is entitled **HOMEMADE BREADMAKING MADE EASY.** Someone has said, "Bread is the staff of life." Yet a *Redbook* magazine survey of 85,000 women

indicated that only _____ in _____

women bake their own bread regularly. While

_____ % feel that homemade yeast bread is the most difficult to prepare, the same survey

discovered the revealing fact that _____% never use any unrefined or natural foods such as whole wheat flour, brown rice, soy beans, honey, or granola. Today's demonstrations will enable you to make your own nutritious homemade bread simply and efficiently.

II. Advantages of Making Homemade Bread

Why take the time and energy to make your own bread when you can easily go to the store and buy it? What are the advantages of good homemade bread? Is white bread as nutritiously healthy as whole grain bread? What about the enriching process — doesn't that solve the problem? These are good questions. Let's explore some answers.

1. **Whole grain breads are an excellent source of dietary fiber.**

Fiber is the _____

portion of _____

cellular material after _____ .

It provides _____ or roughage in the diet.

Fiber assists in preventing the big three killers of:

a. _____

b. _____

c. _____

2. Whole grain breads are an excellent source of B vitamins.

B vitamins assist in _____ the _____ system.

3. Whole grain breads have the natural goodness as packaged by our loving Creator. They are not depleted by processing and artificially enriching them.

The enrichment process adds back at least four essential nutrients to depleted white flour: thiamine, riboflavin, niacin, and iron. Sixteen others generally are not. Some of these additional 16 may play a significant role in health maintenance. Dr. Rodger J. Williams, from the University of Texas, called attention to the deficiencies of enriched white flour in a speech before the National Academy of Science in the fall of 1970. He described experiments with rats who were fed only commercially-enriched white flour.

Within _____ days, _____ of the original _____ rats were dead of malnutrition. In a group of 64 rats fed bread made of flour supplemented with additional vitamins and minerals (plus lysine, an amino acid essential to growth), all but three gained weight and thrived. Whole grains in their natural packaging are an important part of health.

4. Whole grain breads are free from some of the artificial preservatives and additives which may be present in commercially-prepared breads.

5. Homemade whole grain breads are much cheaper.

The average loaf of homemade whole grain bread costs $_____.
The average loaf of whole grain store-bought bread costs $_____.

The monthly difference in bread alone for a family of five is $_____.

6. Whole grain breadmaking is a lost art in today's fast-paced society, and provides a sense of family

_____ and

_____ .

III. *Diet and Disposition*

Recent studies indicate that a good diet with adequate whole grains significantly influences behavior.

A. Diet assists in rehabilitating criminals.

Barbara Reed, Chief Probation Officer in Cuyahoga Falls, Ohio, affirmed that when criminals are switched from junk foods to more fruits, vegetables, and whole grains, their return rate to court after being released from jail is much less.

Carolyn Brown, Executive Director of a residential facility for delinquent children in Berkeley, California, declared, "There is a direct connection between a

_____ , _____

_____ and _____ .

B. "A diet low in whole grains but high in fat and sugar influences thought patterns negatively." This is George Watson's description in *Nutrition and Your Mind.*

Lady #1	Lady #2
High-fat, high-sugar diet	Natural diet of wholesome foods
_____	_____
_____	_____
_____	_____
_____	_____

C. Dr. Ray Williams of the Mayo Clinic in Rochester, Minnesota, discovered a definite relationship between negative behavior and a lack of _thiamine_ in the diet.

Thiamine deficiency produces:

1. _____

2. _____

3. _____

D. Writing almost one hundred years ago, Ellen White, an American pioneer in healthful eating, stated:

> **"Anything that lessens physical strength enfeebles the mind and makes it less capable of discriminating between right and wrong. We become less capable of choosing the good, and have less strength of will to do that which we know to be right."** _Counsels on Diet and Foods_, p. 49.

As you continue to discover the essential principles of healthful eating and put these principles into practice in your life, you will quickly begin to notice the benefits. Your health will improve. Your energy level will increase. Your thinking will become clearer. You will feel more alert and positive about life.

Eating a nutritious, tasty, natural diet will produce both a healthy mind and body. Truly the ancient Scriptures are right when they declare: "Happy (fortunate) are you, O land, when your king is of a noble character and your princes eat for strength and not for drunkenness." Ecclesiastes 10:17 (paraphrase). Eating for strength and not for mere gratification of appetite produces **physical health** and **mental joy**.

During each session we shall add additional basic principles which will not only transform your eating but will revolutionize your way of thinking, enabling you to become a more contented, self-controlled and cheerful person. Jesus said, "I am the bread of life." John 6:48. Good whole grain homemade bread satisfies the nutritional needs of the body, just as Jesus satisfies our inner spiritual needs.

In Our Next Session . . .

MAKING BREAKFAST A BETTER MEAL. In it you will discover how to prepare:

- delicious whole grain cereals
- tasty fruit cobblers
- delightful fresh fruit juices and salads
- healthful, low-cost granola — and many other dishes

You will also learn why:

- breakfast is the most important meal of the day
- many students and businessmen/women experience mid-morning let down
- so many people skip breakfast

We shall look forward to seeing you during the next session. Be sure to attend. It's not too late to invite a friend.

Table 1

Vitamin and Mineral Loss in Processed Flours

VITAMIN or MINERAL	% of Loss
Vitamin B_1 (Thiamine)	86
Vitamin B_2 (Riboflavin)	70
Niacin	86
Iron	84
Vitamin B_6 (Lyridoxine)	60
Folic Acid	70
Pantothenic Acid	54
Biotin	90
Calcium	50
Phosphorous	78
Copper	75
Magnesium	72
Manganese	71

Only vitamins B_1, B_2, niacin, and the mineral iron are added back in the enrichment process. Calculated from *Lesser Known Vitamins in Foods*, J. Am. Diet Association 38:240-243.

Steps to Success in Breadmaking

I. Recipe
    a. Choose a simple, basic recipe.

    b. If you are a beginner in breadmaking, it would be helpful to use soy, gluten, or some unbleached white flour with the whole wheat flour.

II. Yeast
    a. Kinds of yeast:

        i. dry yeast — added directly to dry flour.

        ii. dry active yeast — softened in warm water (110 degrees).

        iii. compressed or fresh yeast — softened in lukewarm water (85 degrees).

    b. Factors that retard yeast:

        i. Salt and fat both retard the growth of the yeast and should not be added to a yeast mixture until it has grown strong and lively by feeding on sugar and starch.

        ii. Too much sugar added directly to the yeast may somewhat retard the action.

        iii. Dry active yeast that is too old will retard the action.

III. Mixing
    a. Mix basic ingredients — water, sweetening, salt, and oil. Add different kinds of flours to change the kind of bread.

    b. Develop the gluten of the wheat flour in the batter by beating thoroughly, then add other kinds of flour.

    c. Bread of fine texture and good flavor is partly the result of thorough kneading after all the ingredients have been combined.

    d. Other ingredients in addition to the flour, like raisins, apricots, caraway seeds, etc., should be added to the basic ingredients while it is still a liquid. Then enough flour is added to obtain a stiff dough.

IV. Kneading
    a. All the flour necessary to keep dough from sticking to your hands should be added at the time of kneading. (A poor job of kneading dough before the first rising cannot be remedied.)

9

b. A good way to knead is to lift the dough and fingers, fold it over and push down with the heel of the hand. Do this over and over until you have a smooth ball.

V. Rising
a. Place dough in oiled bowl. Cover to prevent forming crust.
b. Let rise in warm place (not hot) until double in size (about 1 ½ hours).

VI. Making Loaves
a. Punch down, divide and form into balls.
b. Use approximately 1 to 1 ¼ pounds of dough to each loaf.
c. The loaf will take the shape of the pan so don't fill pans too full or bread will spill over the sides causing cracked, over-browned crusts.
d. Form into loaves and place in bread pan.

VII. Rising in Bread Pans
a. Let rise 45 minutes to 1 hour before baking.
b. When bread is doubled in bulk and ready to bake, dough will retain a dent when pressed lightly.
c. Over-raised bread can fall when it hits the extreme heat, so it is better to bake a little "under" raised than "over" raised.

VIII. Baking
a. Bake in moderate oven 350 degrees F. or 180 degrees C.
b. Bake until thoroughly done — approximately 40 to 45 minutes.
c. Loaves should be golden brown on all sides.
d. Bread should slip out of the pan easily if baked properly.

IX. Cooling
a. Leave uncovered on racks.
b. Cool thoroughly before putting into bags.

X. Storing
a. Homemade bread will keep approximately one week stored in bread box.
b. Bread freezes well. Make several different kinds and freeze.

The Effect of B-Vitamins On The Nerves

Even though only minute quantities of B-vitamins are needed by the body, they form an essential part of the enzyme economy of the tissue cells. Their absence or scarcity causes all cells of the body to suffer. Effects can be seen in the skin, digestive system, heart and blood systems, etc. Perhaps in the nervous system the most troublesome and early signs are noted. The following items point out the importance of abundant B-vitamins in storage in the body.

1. Three groups of chickens were fed diets as follows:

    a. 100% whole wheat flour
    b. enriched white flour
    c. unenriched white flour

The effect of the reduction in B-vitamins caused the 3rd group of chicks to die in 5 days. Those fed on brown flour and enriched flour, both feathered out and gained weight in a normal fashion. The first group had only the barest detectable difference in 5 days, the advantage being in favor of the brown flour group. The chicks fed on the enriched white flour had a high-pitched, rapid chirp. They were untidy in their cage, stepping in their water, then in the flour, making "boots" for their feet. The chicks were high-strung and nervous, often pecking each other, or jittering together in one corner of the cage if a slight noise frightened them. We can conclude that plumpness and the condition of the skin, hair, or feathers are not the only criteria to be used in determining the adequacy of a diet. Cheerfulness, self-control, mental efficiency, and productivity all count in this determination.

2. Certain hyperactive children have become more calm and easier to control when foods poor in B-vitamins, food additives, and rich or irritating foods have been removed from their diets.

3. It has been observed for years that individuals with blood sugar problems, either too high or too low, were often difficult to work with and had wide mood swings. In the metabolism of sugar in the body, B-vitamins are used up. The periodic irritability and emotional instability seen in these persons are typical of a B-vitamin deficiency. As the blood sugar rises, whether from reactive hypoglycemia, diabetes, or from eating largely of refined carbohydrates, B-vitamins are removed from body stores to care for the elevated blood sugar, resulting in a B-vitamin deficiency.

4. Pellagra, pernicious anemia, beri-beri, and all other diseases caused by a B-vitamin deficiency, have nervous or mental symptoms as a part of the disease complex.

ANSWER SHEET
**Session 1: Homemade Breadmaking
Made Easy**

I. Nutrition and Your Health
   a. Six
   b. one third
   c. secondary
   d. 40
   Redbook Magazine survey:
   one, ten; 38, 45

II. Advantages of Making Homemade Bread
   1. undigested, vegetable, digestion; bulk
      a. Heart disease
      b. Cancer
      c. Strokes
   2. stabilizing, nervous
   3. 77, 45, 66
   5. .65(¢), 1.35, 21.00
   6. cohesiveness, security

III. Diet and Disposition
   A. wholesome, nutritious diet, crime
   B. #1: anxious, suspicious, irritable,
         ill-tempered
      #2: relaxed, confident, compatible, happy
   C. 1. irritability
      2. nervousness
      3. depression

Natural Lifestyle Cooking

Session 2

Making Breakfast a Better Meal

Introduction

Would you like to increase your life expectancy by as much as eleven years? What price would you pay for eleven more happy, healthy years? If a formula for longevity could be put into a pill, would you take it? Dr. Lester Breslow, Dean of the School of Health at UCLA made a startling assertion: "It is possible, by following seven basic health guidelines, to increase American life expectancy by eleven years." After conducting extensive research, Dr. Breslow concluded that the seven principles listed below will add years to your life:

1. Avoid tobacco.
2. Limit the use of alcohol.
3. Avoid eating between meals.
4. Get adequate rest (7 to 8 hours per night).
5. Engage in frequent exercise.
6. Remain close to your ideal weight.
7. Eat a good breakfast every day.

In today's class we shall focus on the last of these basic seven health principles — eating a good breakfast. Many people feel too rushed or too tired to eat a good breakfast. Some are not hungry. Others feel they want to lose weight and skipping breakfast is a good way to do it.

In a recent survey it was discovered that only _____ in _____ children have a substantial breakfast. Among the teenage group _____ % of the girls and

_____ % of the boys eat no breakfast at all (Ethel Nelson, M.D., *Century 21 Cookbook*, p. 84). What do these statistics reveal? Is there a relationship between a poor quality breakfast and mental attitudes? Does the typical breakfast of highly-refined cereals, coffee, and doughnuts contribute to the Western world's growing epidemic of heart disease and cancer? What are the advantages of a substantial breakfast? What composes a nutritionally sound morning meal? In today's session we shall explore answers to these questions.

I. The Benefits of a Substantial Breakfast

1. **Classroom Attitudes and Scholastic Achievements Improve**
   One of the classic studies on the benefits of a good breakfast is entitled the *Iowa Breakfast Studies*. This massive study indicated the detrimental effect of skipping breakfast and the positive benefits of eating a good breakfast. In a pilot program conducted by the U.S. Department of Agriculture on 12- to 14-year old boys, the results showed that among the effects were:

   Detrimental —

   a. lowered _____ span

   b. poorer _____ attitudes

   Beneficial —

   a. increased _____ span

   b. positive _____ attitudes

   c. greater _____ ability (memory)

2. **Workers who eat a good breakfast have:**

   a. better _____ toward work

   b. greater _____ on the job

3. **Circadian rhythms or sleep patterns are unbalanced** in people who regularly skip breakfast, which leads to eating _____ at night.

4. **A good breakfast provides essential vitamins and minerals** enabling the body to function at peak energy levels throughout the morning, thus reducing the typical mid-morning _____ and the need for _____ .

II. A Good Breakfast and Your Health!

DIETARY FIBER

Modern medical researchers have concluded that dietary fiber aids in reducing the risk of both heart disease and cancer. Dietary fiber is essential to good health. It is found in fresh fruits, whole grains, bran, beans, carrots, and other natural products. It is that which remains from the plant material and cannot be digested by the enzymes of our gastro-intestinal tract. It is largely cellulose and related substances.

In England, researchers such as Dr. D.P. Burkitt have published their conclusions that a diet high in fiber helps to reduce the transit time of waste materials in the intestines and bowels. This reduced transit time lessens the time of contact, thus reducing the possibility of cancer.

Speaking at a large medical convention in Los Angeles, Dr. Burkitt pointed out that:

a. the transit time of the Bantu native averages _____ hours.

b. the transit time of the average Englishman is from _____ to _____ hours.

In every society in the world where there is a highly refined diet consisting largely of sugars and fats, the bowel cancer rate is unusually high. In those societies where the diet is high in fiber, the bowel cancer rate is low.

When the Japanese move from their villages to the cities, their diet changes from one high in fiber to one that is highly refined and the bowel cancer rates go up.

CEREALS HIGH IN SUGAR

Dr. Ira Shannon and his co-workers at the Veterans Administration Hospital in Houston, Texas, analyzed 78 ready-to-eat breakfast cereals for their overall sugar content. To their amazement, they discovered that 23 of the

cereals proved to be _____ to _____ percent sugar, while 24 of the 78 were a whopping

_____ to_____ percent sugar. This is certainly a good reason to make your own healthful breakfast cereals.

Whole grain cereals provide protein, calcium, iron, trace minerals, B-vitamins, vitamin E in the germ and, of course, fiber in the bran.

EGGS AND COFFEE

What about the traditional breakfast of bacon, eggs, and coffee? Dr. C. Bruce Taylor, professor of Pathology at Northwestern University Medical School, as reported in the *Washington Star*, declared: "The best way for a woman to kill her husband is to feed him one egg per day." He claims that the yolk of an egg contains about all the cholesterol the human body can handle in one day without developing fatty patches in the heart and brain arteries over the years.

Dr. Taylor is an authority on the effects of diet and arteriosclerosis. The Hinsdale Hospital Health Education Department encourages its

patients to eat no more than _____ eggs per week. This, of course, is in harmony with the recommendations of the American Medical Association. This number includes those you would use in cooking. The age-old daily breakfast of bacon and eggs, consisting of enormous levels of high fat is becoming a thing of the past.

Coffee contains an artificial stimulant, caffeine, which has been associated with nervousness, anxiety, muscular tremors, stomach ulcers, heart disease and a host of other medical problems.

BREAKFAST AND DIGESTION

When you get up in the morning, it usually has been between 8 and 12 hours since your last meal. Your glucose or blood sugar level is at its lowest point in the day. Glucose is the basic fuel for the brain and central nervous system. A good breakfast will keep you from being tired and irritable by mid-morning. Since the stomach is rested, there are two real advantages of eating a large, healthy nutritious breakfast.

1. All _____ _____ are

   _____ _____ and the

   _____ is ready to receive more food.

2. _____ _____ have

   been _____ by the

   _____ upon awakening to

   prepare for the thorough _____ of your food.

III. Guidelines for a Good Breakfast

A good breakfast should be:

1. **nutritious** — supplying at least _____

   _____ to _____ _____ of the day's food needs. It should include:

   - one serving of cooked fruit
   - one serving of fresh fruit
   - one serving of a whole grain cereal with milk
   - one/two slices of whole grain bread

2. **appetizing and attractive.**

3. **ready on time allowing adequate time to eat.**

4. **simple and easy to eat.**

5. **a family meal.**
   (Summarized from *Food, Health and Efficiency* by Marion Vollmer, printed by Southern Publishing Association.)

Upon awakening in the morning, why not try this simple routine? Begin your day by thanking God for another day of life. Read a verse from the Bible. Drink a large glass of water. Take a 15-minute walk, then eat a good breakfast. Although it may require getting up a little earlier, the rewards of good heath, a positive mental attitude, and a closer walk with God will be well worth it.

In Our Next Session . . .

PLANNING A BALANCED MENU, we will be discussing cholesterol and its relationship to heart disease and how to avoid unnecessary cholesterol by planning a healthy and balanced menu.

ANSWER SHEET
Session 2: Making Breakfast a Better Meal

Introduction
1, 20, 48, 24

I. **The Benefits of a Substantial Breakfast**

1. Detrimental	Beneficial
a. attention	a. attention
b. classroom	b. classroom
	c. learning

2. a. attitudes
   b. efficiency
3. late
4. tiredness, coffee

II. **A Good Breakfast and Your Health!**
   a. 34
   b. 80, 120
   Cereals High In Sugar
     20, 25; 25, 40
   Eggs and Coffee
     three
   Breakfast and Digestion
     1. previous meals, well digested, stomach
     2. Digestive juices, secreted, stomach, digestion

III. **Guidelines for a Good Breakfast**
   1. one third, one half

Table 2

Sugar Content of Commercially Available Breakfast Cereals

Cereal Product	% Sugar Content
Shredded Wheat (large)	1.2
Shredded Wheat (spoon size)	1.6
Cheerios	2.7
Puffed Rice	2.8
Wheat Chex	3.5
Uncle Sam Cereal	3.6
Grape Nut Flakes	3.9
Puffed Wheat	4.2
Post Toasties	5.8
Product 19	5.8
Corn Total	5.8
Peanut Butter	6.3
Corn Flakes (Kroger)	6.6
Grape Nuts	7.7
Corn Chex	8.4
Alpen	8.5
Crispy Rice	8.8
Wheaties	8.9
Corn Flakes (Food Club)	9.1
Total	9.4
Rice Chex	10.3
Special K	10.8
Crisp Rice	10.9
Concentrate	12.3
Rice Crispies (Kellogg)	12.9
Corn Flakes (Kellogg)	14.2
Buck Wheat	15.1
Brown Sugar-Cinnamon Frosted Mini Wheats	16.3
Life	17.0
Team	17.0
Granola	17.2
Sugar Frosted Corn Flakes	17.4
Granola (with dates)	17.7
Granola (with raisins)	18.3

40% Bran Flakes (Kellogg) 18.3
40% Bran Flakes (Post) 18.8
Raisin Bran (Skinner) 18.9
Heartland (with raisins) 19.1
100% Bran 19.2
All Bran 21.6
Granola (with almonds & filberts) 22.6
Fortified Oat Flakes 23.4
Raisin Bran (Kellogg) 24.7
Super Sugar Chex 25.3
Heartland 26.3
Sugar Frosted Flakes 30.8
Bran Buds 32.3
Sugar Sparkled Corn Flakes 24.0
Frosted Mini Wheats 34.0
Sugar Pops 40.7
Alpha Bits 40.9
Sir Grapefellow 43.8
Cap'n Crunch 44.1
Crunch Berries 44.4
Super Sugar Crisp 45.2
Orange Quangaroos 45.3
Quisp 45.5
Cocoa Puffs 46.5
Vanilly Crunch 46.5
Frankenberry 46.6
Cocoa Krispies 46.7
Kaboom 46.8
Frosted Flakes 46.9
Baron Von Redberry 47.3
Count Chocula 47.9
Froot Loops 47.9
Boo Berry 48.5
Pink Panther 50.5
Honeycomb 51.6
Cinnamon Crunch 53.5
Cocoa Pebbles 54.1
Apple Jacks 55.5
Fruity Pebbles 56.2
King Vitaman 61.6
Sugar Smacks 63.7
Super Orange Crisp 70.8

Journal of Dentistry for Children.

Natural Lifestyle Cooking

Session 3

Planning a Balanced Menu

Introduction

The evidence is mounting! Heart disease, America's number-one killer can be to a larger degree prevented, and diet plays a significant factor in reducing our risk of death from a heart attack. Myron Coenick, Director of the Institute of Human Nutrition at Columbia University, stated: "The evidence for a relationship between fat and cholesterol and coronary artery disease, cancer, and diabetes has become so solid that only the most diehard would deny it." *US News and World Report*, January 20, 1986.

The American diet is approximately 40% fat. The Senate Select Subcommittee on Nutrition recommended that Americans reduce the fat in their

diet by at least _____% to a maximum of _____%. They also recommended that

cholesterol intake be reduced to _____ mg. per day. One egg contains a whopping 250 mg. With 55% of all deaths in the United States coming from coronary heart disease, and one in five American men dying of a heart attack before the age of 60, the government is alarmed. For this reason, the leading health authorities in the land are calling for a drastic reduction in the amount of fat we consume.

I. Cholesterol Facts

Cholesterol is a fatty substance manufactured by the body. It is also present in all foods of animal origin. Vegetable products do not contain cholesterol. Some contain limited amounts of fat which the body may use to produce cholesterol, but only animal products contain cholesterol which is ingested directly. Most cholesterol enters the blood and is carried around in packets called _____ _____. These microscopic-sized particles are made up largely of fat, cholesterol, and protein. They act like _____ .

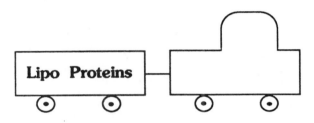

Trucking Cholesterol Away From Local Scene

There is a problem when _____ cholesterol is not _____ away. It is _____ on the_____ walls leading to_____ of the _____ and_____ heart disease.

Unobstructed Artery

Partially-obstructed Artery

Blocked off Artery

Polyunsaturated fats are fats of _____ origin. Most are liquid at room temperature.

Saturated fats are usually of _____ origin. These hard fats are mostly solids at room temperature and tend to elevate blood cholesterol.

Use less saturated fats	Replace with polyunsaturated fat
Meat fats	Sunflower oil
Shortening	Corn oil
Butter	Soy oil
Cream	Cottonseed oil
Whole Milk	Any products containing vegetable oils: soy milk, nut milks
Egg yolk	Egg replacers
Chocolate	Carob

II. Relationship Between a High-Fat Diet and Coronary Heart Disease

Recent studies have evaluated a nation's fat content in its diet and then compared this fat content to the rate at which people are dying from coronary heart disease. The results are similar worldwide. This similarity, despite cultural differences, genetic variants, and changing environments is truly remarkable. The simple principle is: if a nation has a diet high in saturated fats, it also has an extremely high rate of coronary heart disease.

FINNISH STUDIES AT A MENTAL HOSPITAL

Group 1	Group 2
Skim milk	Whole milk
Vegetable oil	Animal fats
Soft margarine	Butter
Low-fat	Average Finnish high-fat diet

At the end of six years, death rates from

coronary heart disease were_____ as

_____ in the group on a _____ -fat diet.

The groups were then switched for six more

years. The results: The situation _____

itself when the two groups_____ diets.

L.A. VETERANS ADMINISTRATION HOSPITAL STUDY

The veterans in Los Angeles were split into two groups with each being assigned a different cafeteria. In one, polyunsaturated fats were used instead of saturated animal fats. In the other the normal high-fat American diet was served. At

the end of eight years the group on the_____-

_____ diet suffered a dramatic _____
in heart attacks.

CALIFORNIA — SEVENTH-DAY ADVENTIST STUDIES

Fifty thousand Seventh-day Adventists were surveyed by a team of University researchers. They completed extremely thorough health questionnaires. Their personal medical records were carefully examined. The health statistics of these Adventists were then compared to the general California population.

Vegetarian Adventist men, carefully following a low-fat dietary regime and on an overall balanced lifestyle program, had an overwhelming advantage over their Californian counterparts. The studies revealed that the

Adventist men lived _____ years longer

than their non-Adventist counterparts. This was

an advantage of_____to_____ in

_____ heart attacks. In other words, for every eight Americans who had a heart attack, only one Adventist had one.

III. How to Evaluate Your Personal Risk of a Heart Attack

Medical researchers recognize that no one factor usually causes a heart attack. Most list approximately ten risk factors contributing to a heart attack. Let's review these major risk factors. As we do, place a check in the box beside any risk factor which applies to you.

Risk Factor	Place Check Here
1. Male	❑
2. Hereditary factors (it runs in the family)	❑
3. Little physical activity (no organized exercise program)	❑
4. Inner stress	❑
5. Elevated blood cholesterol (over 200 mg.)	❑
6. High blood pressure	❑
7. Overweight (more than 10 lbs.)	❑
8. Cigarette smoking	❑
9. Coffee drinking (more than 3 cups per day)	❑
10. Insufficient sleep (Less than 6 hrs. per night consistently)	❑

As few as two risk factors indicate the need of dietary control. Three or four risk factors indicate a good possibility of a heart attack, while over five necessitate immediate attention. It is interesting to note that six of the ten have some relationship to diet. Which ones are they? Why? The good news is that it is possible to do something about 8 of the above 10 risk factors. We can make choices to change faulty lifestyle habit patterns into positive, health-building ones.

IV. *Dietary Control of Cholesterol*

Since dietary fat (amount and type) is directly related to coronary heart disease, a blood cholesterol of over 250 mg. presents four times the risk of a heart attack than one less than 200 mg.

The following practical steps will help lower the blood cholesterol:

1. Change the type of fat from _____

   to_____ .

2. Use nut milks, soy milk or skim milk.

   Limit the use of_____ _____

   and_____ .

3. Use _____ sparingly.

4. Lower or eliminate _____ _____

   or _____ _____ .

5. Limit the use of_____ _____.

6. Control the intake of sugars in all forms (white, brown, raw, etc.).

7. Eat a wide variety of whole grains, fruits, nuts and vegetables.

V. *A Brief Guide to the Basic Four Food Groups of Balanced Eating*

U.S. News and World Report interviewed a number of experts in nutrition and published their responses in an article entitled "Experts' Recipes for a Healthy Life," January 20, 1986. Michael Jacobson, Executive Director for the Center for Science in the Public Interest, stated: "The consensus is that Americans should be eating less fat, cholesterol, sodium, and refined sugars and eating more starch and dietary fiber. The best foods for you are beans, grains, fresh fruits, vegetables, and low-fat dairy, meat and poultry foods. The worst foods for you are hot dogs, fatty steaks, cheeseburgers, fried foods, soda pop, most pastries, and ice cream."

Walter Mertz, Director of the Agriculture Departments, Human Nutrition Research Center, added, "The rule should be — everything in balance . . ."

A balanced vegetarian diet includes a wide variety of foods from the food groups listed below:

Basic Food Group	Servings per day (please write in)
1. Bread and cereal group (including varying types of milks)	_____
2. Vegetable group (cooked or raw)	_____
3. Fruits (canned or fresh)	_____
4. Proteins	_____

VI. *Daily Eating Guide for a Balanced Menu*

Breakfast

1 serving whole grain cereal, cooked cereal or other main dish

1 to 2 pieces of whole wheat toast

1 serving fresh fruit

1 serving cooked fruit (canned applesauce, peaches, etc.)

1 serving milk or soy milk

Dinner

1 to 2 servings carbohydrate

1 to 2 servings cooked vegetables (beans, corn, peas, etc.)

1 to 2 servings raw vegetables (salads — tossed, cabbage, carrot)

1 to 2 servings protein

optional: bread

Supper

Soups and crackers — or

fruit and toast — or

sandwiches and fruit

Our loving Creator has given us an abundance of natural foods to sustain life and prolong health. After creating the amazing variety of fruits, nuts, grains, and vegetables, He declared: "Ye may freely eat." Genesis 2:16.

As you make wise selections from these basic four food groups, you may eat until your heart is content. Food is meant to be enjoyed. The healthier you eat, the more you will enjoy it and the longer you will live to continue to enjoy it.

In Our Next Session . . .

ADEQUATE PROTEIN INEXPENSIVELY: THE ADVANTAGES OF A VEGETARIAN DIET, we will discuss how to take the practical steps toward vegetarianism. We shall present tasty, nutritious, low-fat, high-protein recipes. You may be surprised at the wide variety of nutritious vegetarian protein dishes available. We will see you next week.

ANSWER SHEET
Session 3: Planning a Balanced Menu

Introduction
10, 30, 300

I. Cholesterol Facts
lipo proteins, trucks
excess, trucked, deposited, arterial, hardening, arteries, coronary
vegetable, animal

II. Relationship Between a High-Fat Diet and Coronary Heart Disease
Finnish Studies at a Mental Hospital
twice, high, high; reversed, switched
L.A. Veterans Administration Hospital Study
high-fat, increase
California — Seventh-day Adventist Studies
seven; eight, one, reducing

IV. Dietary Control of Cholesterol
1. animal, vegetable
2. whole milk, cheeses
3. eggs
4. flesh foods, meat products
5. fried foods

V. A Brief Guide to the Basic Four Food Groups of Balanced Eating
1. 2 to 3
2. 3 to 4
3. 3 to 4
4. 2 to 3

Low-Cholesterol, Low-Fat, Low-Sugar Diet

Type of Food	Foods Allowed	Foods to Avoid
Beverages (non-dairy)	Unsweetened fruit and vegetable juices, cereal, coffees (Pioneer, Postum, etc.).	Alcohol of all kinds. Coffee, tea, and most carbonated beverages.
Breads	Whole grain breads: whole wheat, rye, corn, and mixtures, **not** containing whole milk, eggs, or animal fat.	Most commercially-made white breads, cookies, pastries, and crackers.
Cereals	All cooked cereals and whole grain products. We recommend whole wheat macaroni, noodles, and spaghetti. Dry cereals of granola type.	Most dry cereals, as they contain considerable sugar.
Fats	All vegetable oils; soft sunflower or corn oil margarines; homemade mayonnaise; peanut butter, olives. All nuts and seeds (pumpkin, sesame, sunflower).	Butter and cream; lard; hydrogenated margarines and shortenings; bacon and meat drippings; cream sauces and gravies unless specially made of polyunsaturated fats; commercial mayonnaise.
Fruit	Any fresh, frozen, or dried fruits or juices. Canned fruits should be water packed.	Sweetened fruits and juices.
Meats	Meat substitutes made of vegetable protein may be used. Bakos. Legumes such as beans, peas, lentils, garbanzos will adequately substitute for meat.	Pork and pork products; egg yolk; all shellfish; poultry skin; all organ meats; luncheon meat products, such as hot dogs and sandwich meats; regular hamburger; most frozen or packaged dinners.
Soups	Meat-free vegetable soups; soups made with soy, nut, or skim milk; packaged dehydrated soups.	All others.
Sweets	Natural dried fruits such as raisins, dates, figs (up to 1 teaspoon per day of honey, sugars, or syrups).	Cakes, candies, jams, jellies, preserves unless dietetic, ice cream, milk, sodas, and shakes.
Vegetables	Any fresh, frozen, or canned (check for sugar).	Buttered, creamed, or fried (unless in vegetable oil).

U.S. Dietary Goals

1. Increase carbohydrate consumption to account for **55** to **60%** of the (caloric) intake.

2. Reduce overall fat to **30%** of energy intake.

3. Reduce saturated fat to **10%** of total energy intake.

4. Reduce cholesterol to about **300 mg.** per day.

5. Reduce sugar to about **15%** of total energy intake.

6. Reduce salt intake to about **3 grams** per day.

Food Selection

The goals suggest the following changes in food selection and preparation:

1. Increase consumption of fruits and vegetables and whole grain.

2. Decrease consumption of meat and increase consumption of poultry and fish.

3. Decrease consumption of foods high in fat and partially substitute polyunsaturated fat for saturated fat.

4. Substitute nonfat milk for whole milk.

5. Decrease consumption of butterfat, eggs, and other high-cholesterol sources.

6. Decrease consumption of sugar and foods high in sugar content.

7. Decrease consumption of salt and foods high in salt content.

Know Your Condiments

1. **Stimulating Condiments:** These include cayenne red pepper, white and black peppers, mustard, horse-radish, and certain kinds of paprika where the seeds of the plant are included. They are irritating and stimulating, producing a sense of heat in the stomach. Severe inflammation may result from repeated ingestion of these products. Hungarian paprika, though obtained from the same botanical family as the red pepper, is markedly sweet. Pimiento, or Spanish paprika, is almost devoid of pungency.

2. **Aromatic Spices:** Allspice, anise, caraway, cinnamon, cloves, coriander, cumin seed, ginger, mace, and nutmeg are obtained from plant sources. They have a fragrant odor and slightly stimulating properties. Ginger is one of the leading aromatic spices and is stronger than some of the others. Cloves are also among the stronger aromatics. Cinnamon is a mild heart stimulant. Nutmeg has slightly aromatic properties, but its oil is used chiefly as a flavoring oil. Mace is similar to nutmeg and is obtained from the surrounding membrane of the nutmeg.

3. **Sweet Herbs:** Bay leaf, dillseed, fennel, marjoram, saffron, sage, savory, thyme, mint parsley. The greater share of these herbs exert a slight antiseptic property, thyme especially so. They are not irritating to the mucous membrane. There are also mixed spices on the market, such as poultry seasoning, which contains sage, marjoram, thyme, savory, pepper, nutmeg, and allspice.

Condiments at a Glance

Irritating, stimulating, harmful

Cayenne pepper, Chili powder, Horse-radish, Mustard, Pepper (black or white)

Strongly aromatic, irritating

Cloves, Ginger, Paprika (Hungarian)

Slightly irritating

Allspice, Anise, Cassia, Cinnamon, Cumin seed, Mace, Nutmeg

Sweet herbs, not irritating

Bay leaf, Caraway seed, Celery salt, Celery seed, Chives, Dillseed, Fennel, Kitchen bouquet, Marjoram, Mint, Onion salt, Paprika (Spanish type, highly colored), Parsley, Peppermint, Saffron, Sage, Savory, Spearmint, Thyme, Tumeric, Wintergreen

INGREDIENTS OF MIXED SPICES

Poultry Seasoning	Curry (Foreign)	Curry (American)
Allspice	Black pepper	Cinnamon
Marjoram	Cayenne pepper	Cloves
Nutmeg	Cinnamon	Coriander
Sage	Cloves	Ginger
Savory	Nutmeg	Mace
		Nutmeg
		Pepper
		Tumeric

From *Homemakers' Cookbook and Guide to Nutrition*, by Esther L. Gardner, M.A., Dietitian, Director of School of Dietetics, College of Medical Evangelists; Daisy Schluntz, M.S., Head of the Home Economics Department at Walla Walla College; Ruth Little, Dietitian, White Memorial Hospital; Mary Turner, Dietitian.

Natural Lifestyle Cooking

Session 4

Adequate Protein Inexpensively: The Advantages of a Vegetarian Diet

Introduction

A growing number. of Americans are either limiting the amount of meat they eat or are discarding meat altogether. According to a recent survey, some seven million people claim they are vegetarians in the United States. The figures have jumped by 300% in the last generation. Vegetarianism has steadily grown in popularity.

The word "vegetarian" is not derived from the word "vegetable" as is commonly supposed — it comes from the Latin word "vegus" which means "whole, sound, fresh, lively." Vegetarians are those who exclude eating meat from their diet for moral, ethical, or health reasons. Vegetarians don't necessarily do all their shopping in health food stores. Many shop at ordinary grocery stores and just skip the meat.

Throughout history, many of the world's brightest minds and most creative personalities have been vegetarians. George Bernard Shaw, English playwright, could not bring himself to "eat the flesh of dead corpses." Two of the world's longest living civilizations, the Hunzas in the Himalayas, and the Otomai Indians of South America are predominantly vegetarians.

According to the National Academy of Sciences, National Research Council, which publishes the Recommended Daily Allowances for U.S. Food, "All but the most restricted vegetarian diets are nutritionally safe . . . . The most important safeguard for the average vegetarian consumer is great variety in the diet . . . . " As long as vegetarians eat a wide variety of fruits, nuts, grains, and vegetables they will normally receive adequate protein.

In this class, you will discover how to prepare delicious low-cholesterol, vegetarian protein dishes. You may have wondered, "Does the vegetarian diet provide adequate protein? What advantages does a vegetarian diet have over a meat diet? Is vegetable protein complete? Does it really matter if a protein source is complete or not? How much protein does one really need?" During this session you will find the answers to these questions.

I. Fundamental Facts About Protein

Proteins are composed of _____

_____ . The body manufactures amino acids from the foods we eat. Those amino acids which cannot be produced by the body are called essential amino acids. Of the 22 known amino acids, nine cannot be produced by the body and must be present in the food we eat. These essential amino acids are all present in meat. They can also be obtained from a variety of vegetable proteins eaten in combination with grains and nuts.

Facts to Remember About Proteins

It is not the amino acid content of a simple protein source that is important but that of the entire _____ _____ .

If a diet has adequate calories and contains a wide variety of fruits, grains, and vegetables, the _____ is usually _____ .

Dr. Frederick Stare, Nutritionist and Professor at Harvard University, stated in his study of protein foods, published in the *American Journal of Public Health*: "As long as this country has access to a plentiful supply of calories and a variety of whole grain cereals and legumes, it is _____ _____ that impairment of health from protein deficiency will ever occur."

Complete vegetarian protein combinations include:

- All grains and legumes
- All grains and milk products
- All legumes and seeds
- Milk products and either seeds or legumes.

Examples might include: Rice-bean casserole, wheat bread with baked beans, bean or pea curry on rice, corn tortillas and beans, lentil soup with bread, cereal with milk, cashew nut roast with bread, wheat-soy bread, and many others.

Protein Requirements

Women:	44-50 grams per day
Men:	52-56 grams per day
Children:	23-35 grams per day

Vegetarian protein and animal protein both can be complete proteins. The quality of vegetarian protein is easier to break down since it does not contain the fat by-products as does animal protein.

II. Why Be a Vegetarian?

What advantages do vegetarians have? From a health standpoint, is it worth it to markedly reduce your meat intake and eventually cut it out altogether?

Decrease Your Risk of a Heart Attack

Each year there are close to 600,000 deaths in the U.S. due to coronary artery disease. This accounts for 55% of all deaths. One important key in reducing heart attack deaths is reducing the fat in the diet. As America has become more health conscious and has reduced its fat intake in the last 15 years, deaths from heart disease have been

_____ in the United States by _____ to _____%.

In Japan, Greece, and Italy where levels of blood cholesterol are _____ compared with the average American levels, the rate of heart disorders is _____ than in the United States.

John M. Chapman of UCLA School of Medicine states: "A cholesterol-lowering diet in older men has resulted in significantly

_____ heart attack death rates.

Decrease Your Risk of Cancer

"There is overwhelming evidence that cancer is related to the environment and diet is a factor, perhaps the major environmental factor," said D.M. Hegsted, Associate Director for Research of Harvard University's Research Center (*Chicago Tribune*, August 10, 1983).

British epidimiologist, Richard Doll, believes food is number one in accounting for 35% of all tumors. Dr. Gio B. Gori, Deputy Director of the National Institute, Division of the Causes of Cancer, believes that _____% of cancer in women and _____ % of cancer in men are the result of a _____ _____ .

To reduce the risks of cancer, eliminate or greatly reduce:
• all visible _____ ; _____ products
• excessive_____ _____ foods
• highly _____ foods

The cancer prevention diet includes:
• whole grains, _____ _____
• leafy green vegetables, _____ _____
• fresh fruits _____
• nuts, _____

Decreased Risk of Animal to Man Communicable Diseases

Salmonellosis, brucellosis, and trichinosis may be transmitted from animal to man. Of more than 200 communicable diseases of animals, 100 are considered infectious to man and 80 are transmitted naturally between vertebrate animals and man. Commenting on Salmonellosis, a bacterial disease which causes vomiting, nausea, and diarrhea, the special issue of the *Life and Health* magazine, page 16, stated: "As long as we use _____ _____ it is a losing battle."

Decreased Risk of the Harmful Effects of Pesticides

Meat contains concentrated pesticide levels.

Meat contains _____ _____ more pesticides than vegetable foods (Kay S. Nelson, M.P.H., paper entitled *Vegetarianism*, p. 1).

Increased Endurance

The ideal diet should not only reduce the risk of disease but give us the greatest "go power" possible. Per-Olaf Astrand, M.D., conducted a study of Swedish men to determine the best diet for athletes. In the study, athletes were given a bicycle endurance test to discover their maximum exercise time.

Bicycle Endurance Test	
Diet	**Exercise time**
1. Meat and Protein diet	= _____ minutes
2. Mixed fuel diet (protein & carbohydrate)	= _____ minutes
3. Vegetarian diet	= _____ minutes

The group on the vegetarian diet lasted nearly three times longer than those on the meat diet.

Improved Use of Land and Resources

1. An acre of land planted in soybeans can produce_____times as much protein as animals grazing on the same land.

2. A pound of beef costs_____ times as much to produce as a pound of non-flesh protein.

3. According to one estimate, feed raised on one acre of land and converted into beef will fill the protein needs of a single person for _____ days. But soybeans raised on the same acre can fill his needs for _____ years.

Common Sense Steps to Becoming a Vegetarian

1. Cut "empty" calories (sugars and visible fats) at least in half.

2. Increase your intake of all four basic food groups.

3. Experiment with a wide selection of vegetarian protein dishes until you discover a few your family really enjoys.

4. Substitute these tasty, nutritious vegetarian dishes for your normal meat dishes at least twice a week.

5. During a transition period, meat analogs from companies like Worthington Foods, Morning Star Farms, Loma Linda Foods, Cedar Lake Foods and others may be helpful.

6. When making the change, begin by cutting out the meat high in saturated fats such as pork, marbled steaks, hamburgers, hot dogs, etc., using primarily fish and chicken.

7. Since lifestyle change is best achieved gradually, give yourself a period of three to six months to make the complete transition.

8. Your taste buds will begin to adapt as you develop a new taste for wholesome foods such as nut roasts, peas, beans, lentils, barley, soya-protein and gluten meat substitutes.

The vegetarian diet is not new. It dates back to the Garden of Eden. It was God's original diet for the human race. This world needs a little more of the Eden life — a life of health, harmony and happiness; a life of inner peace, physical well-being, and a closeness with our Creator. In the hectic pace of 20th century living, the diet from nature's pantry will strengthen both our minds and bodies.

In Our Next Session . . .

SIMPLE, HEALTHFUL DESSERTS, we will discuss how to prepare delicious healthful desserts which are low in sugar. We will see you then.

ANSWER SHEET
Session 4: Adequate Protein Inexpensively: The Advantages of a Vegetarian Diet

I. **Fundamental Facts About Protein**
amino acids
Facts to Remember About Proteins
daily menu; protein, adequate; highly unlikely

II. **Why Be a Vegetarian?**
Decrease Your Risk of a Heart Attack
reduced, 15, 20; low, lower; reducing
Decrease Your Risk of Cancer
30, 40; poor diet
To reduce the risks of cancer . . .
fats, animal; high sugar; refined
The cancer prevention diet includes:
wheat, barley, oats, rye, etc.
carrots, potatoes, beets, corn, etc.
dried fruits, etc.
seeds, beans, etc.
Decreased Risk of Animal to Man Communicable Diseases
animal products
Decreased Risk of the Harmful Effects of Pesticides
14 times
Increased Endurance
Bicycle Endurance Test: 60, 120, 180
Improved Use of Land and Resources
1. 10
2. 4
3. 77; 6.1

Protein Content of Common Foods

Food Item	Amount	Amount of Protein
Whole Wheat Flour	1 cup	8 - 10 grams
White Flour	1/2 cup	6 - 10 grams
Brewer's Yeast	1/2 cup	50 grams
Eggs	1	6 grams
Milk	1 cup	8 grams
Skim Milk	7/8 cup	7 grams
Soy Milk	7/8 cup	7 grams
Cottage Cheese	1/2 cup	20 grams
Soy Beans	1/2 cup	20 grams
Peanut Butter	2 tablespoons	9 grams
Cooked Cereals	3/4 cup	10 - 18 grams
Navy & Lima Beans	1 cup	6 - 8 grams
Bread	1 slice	2 grams
Nuts	1/2 cup	14 - 22 grams
Oatmeal	1 cup	5 grams
Collards	1 cup	5 grams
Lentils	1 cup	5 grams
Prunes	1 cup	3 grams
Frozen Peas	1 cup	5 grams
CHOPPED NUTS		
Almonds	1/3 cup	7 grams
Cashews	1 3/4 cup	7 grams
Peanuts	2 tablespoons	7 grams
Pecans	2/3 cup	7 grams
Walnuts	1/2 cup	7 grams
WORTHINGTON FOODS		
Dinner Entree or Numete	2 ounces	7 grams
Protose	1 ounce	7 grams
Sandwich Spread	2 ounces (approx.)	7 grams
Soy Beans/Sauce	2 ounces	7 grams

Protein Requirements Daily: Men — 70 grams; Women — 60 grams; Ages 1-12 — 40 grams. The larger the frame, the more protein required. Authorities differ as to daily requirement.

Natural Lifestyle Cooking

Session 5

Simple, Healthful Desserts

Introduction

Recently a group of dieticians published a pamphlet on the harmful effects of excessive sugar consumption. They begin with this fascinating sentence: "Judging by the size of America's sugar bowl, it really ought to be a sweet world." Someone has said, "Every day in America is sweeter than the day before," and it is! According to a survey by the U.S. Department of Agriculture, Americans eat approximately 3,500,000 pounds of candy each year. That's about 16 lbs. for every man, woman, and child in the country. This is only the beginning of the story. America's sweet tooth gets longer each year. Our craving for sweets seems more intense each passing decade. Each American consumes approximately 120 lbs. of sugar per year. In the last 170 years, the increase in sugar consumption has been remarkable.

- In 1822 the average American ate _____ teaspoons per day.
- In 1890 the average American ate _____ teaspoons per day.
- In 1905 the average American ate _____ teaspoons per day.
- In 1974 the average American ate _____ teaspoons per day.
- In the 1990s the average American will eat approximately _____ teaspoons per day.

I. Where is All This Sugar Coming From?

Food	Amount	Teaspoons of Sugar
Plain Chocolate Candy Bar*	1 small	6
Chocolate Fudge	1 1/4" square	4
Chewing Gum	1 piece	1/2
Life Saver	1	1/3
Glazed Donut	1	6
Ice cream	3 scoops	12
Soft Drink	12 oz.	8
Milk Shake	1 pint	15
Banana Split	Medium/large	24
Fruit Pie	1 slice	10
Canned Fruit	1 serving	3
Brownies	3" diameter	3

*Candy averages from 75-85% sugar. Popular candy bars weighing five ounces usually contain 15-20 teaspoons of sugar.

Most people are not aware of the large amounts of sugar they are eating because it is hidden in the foods they eat. The common conception is: "Someone else must be getting my share. Certainly I am not eating that much sugar." A more careful analysis indicates that most of us are. Even some foods promoted as "health foods" have large amounts of sugar. Nature Valley "Fruit and Nut Granola" is 29% sugar, while Country Morning "Breakfast Cereal" is 31% sugar. Even General Food's "Raisin Bran" runs at 30.4% sugar. What could be more healthy than something called "Apple Jacks"? There is no problem with the apples! The problem is with the enormous amount of added sugar. Closer examination reveals that Apple Jacks are 54% sugar. What is all this sugar doing to our bodies? How does it affect us? Is excessive sugar consumption all that bad?

II. *Health Hazards of a High-Sugar Diet*

"Highly refined sugar contains no nutrients except sucrose which is digested rapidly and the products are readily absorbed into the system. The fast rate of absorption is the reason why sugar has a reputation of being a quick energy food" (SDA Dietetic Association Pamphlet entitled *Sugar*, p. 2).

There are several problems, however, with this quick absorption of sucrose. Since carbohydrates require a number of B-vitamins for the body to process them, and sugar contains no B-vitamins, the body must draw on its reserves, leaving the possibility of a vitamin B deficiency. High sugar intake has also been associated with obesity, tooth decay, heart disease, diabetes, infection, and irritability. Let's examine these five health-destroying effects of excessive sugar more closely.

1. Obesity

- The average American gets 20% of his calories from the 120 lbs. of sugar he/she eats each year.

- Many people find it easier to over eat refined, concentrated foods.

- Sugar calories not used by the body

  are_____ as _____ .

- Since obesity contributes to heart disease, sugar can be a major culprit.

2. Tooth Decay

- Sugar is easily fermented by bacteria in the mouth.

- Experimental animals on a high-sugar diet are observed to have blocked fluid movement in the canals of the tooth, causing rapid deterioration.

- Due to the effects of World War II, Norway had a significant reduction in its supply of sugar. This decrease in sugar supply caused a reduction in sugar consumption which continued from 1939 to 1945.

During the War years, a _____% reduction in tooth decay was noted.

In Alaska, an amazing _____% increase in tooth decay was reported by Dr. T.J. Pyle, Dental Supervisor, one year after opening the student snack bar canteen in which 28,000 candy bars were sold.

3. Heart Disease

Although there are many risk factors contributing to coronary artery disease, excessive sugar consumption has been implicated as one possible risk factor.

- Dr. John Yudkin's studies at the University of London found that men who suffered heart attacks ate

  _____ as much _____ in their diet.

- Investigators also discovered that

  _____ and _____together tend to elevate fatty substances much higher than either one alone.

4. Hypoglycemia: Low Blood Sugar

Many physicians are currently leaning toward the idea that America's eating of excessive sugar, especially between meals, tends to cause the blood sugar levels to rapidly rise, then fall quickly below the normal levels. The corresponding high of quick energy is followed by a corresponding low of tiredness and lethargy. This is true of all stimulants.

5. Infection: Susceptibility to Disease

Another important factor to consider is the relationship between sugar intake and the ability of the body to fight off disease. When there is danger of infection, the white blood cells increase in number in the blood stream. These soldiers of the body destroy bacteria, the infection causing agent. But when the blood sugar level goes up, they become sluggish and cannot

39

destroy as many bacteria. Studies done by Loma Linda University indicate there is a significant temporary decrease in the ability of certain white blood cells, the phagocytes, to destroy bacteria after a person eats a large amount of sugar at one time.

Normal levels of white blood cell activity do not return until _____ to _____ hours later.

Effect of Sugar Intake on the Ability of White Blood Cells (WBC) to Destroy Bacteria		
Teaspoons of sugar eaten at one time by an average adult	Number of bacteria destroyed by each WBC in 30 min.	Percentage decrease in ability to destroy bacteria
0	14	0
6	10	25
12	5.5	60
18	1	85
24	1	92

Children who eat many sweets are particularly vulnerable to colds and infections. Sugars also appear to be habit forming; the more a person eats, the more they want. This presents a problem since sugar is replacing the more nutritious, balanced foods.

6. Irritability

"Excessive sugar and the lack of vitamin B complex and certain minerals result in the incomplete metabolism of sugar to carbon dioxide and cause pyruvic acid build up with neutralization of _____ ____ resulting in

_____ .

(Ethel Nelson, MD., *Century 21 Cookbook*).

"The willful or ignorant ingestion of these sweets is a great physiological diservice" (Dr. U.D. Register, Loma Linda University).

Why Not Substitute Artificial Sweets With Natural Ones?

Replace the foods in the left-hand column with the ones in the right-hand column:

Chocolate Cake _____

Chocolate Chip Cookies _____

Glazed Donuts _____

Soda Pop _____

Hard Candy _____

Sweet Pies _____

Ice Cream _____

The Bottom Line

Nutritional research continues to produce evidence that the imbalance in the American diet is causing an alarming increase in degenerative diseases. Our sugar and fat consumption is far too high. Dr. Rodger J. Williams, a biochemist who has spent thirty years in research on the nutrition of a single cell, observes: "Malnutrition — unbalanced or inadequate nutrition — at the cellular level should be thought of as a major cause of human disease. This seems crystal clear to me." This distinguished scientist, the discoverer of pantothenic acid, one of the B-vitamins, and former president of the American Chemical Society, makes a significant point here. Malnutrition occurs whenever the cells are deprived of essential vitamins, minerals, carbohydrates, and proteins.

Our body was designed to assimilate the nutrients from a wide variety of wholesome foods. It was not designed for "junk foods" high in fat and sugar and refined artificially. One of the reasons scores of children, youth, and adults are so often hungry and constantly eating without being satisfied is because of what some nutritionists call "hidden hunger" — the body's craving for wholesome foods.

The Joy of Natural Lifestyle Cooking

As you feed your family wholesome nutritious meals, they will be **really** satisfied. The constant nibbling to fill up that "empty hole" will be replaced with a sense of satisfied fullness. Your family will anticipate meals, enjoy them, and reap the benefits of good health.

The ancient Scriptures declare: "Beloved, above all things, I pray that you would prosper and be in health as your soul prospers" (3 John 2). There is another form of "hidden hunger." Every human being has it. It is the hunger for God. There is a God-shaped vacuum within each of our hearts that only our Creator can satisfy. Humans are physical, mental, and spiritual beings. Health consists of physical well-being, mental alertness, and spiritual harmony or peace.

Our wish for you is a life of abundant physical health filled with zest, vitality, and energy; a life of mental joy, inner peace, and happy relationships with those around you and spiritual openness with the God who created you and longs to be your Best Friend.

If the material covered in *Natural Lifestyle Cooking* has been helpful to you, would you please let us know? It would mean a lot to us to hear from you. You may write to:

Creation Enterprises International
P.O. Box 274
Siloam Springs, Arkansas 72761
USA

ANSWER SHEET
Session 5: Simple, Healthful Desserts

Introduction
  2; 10; 20; 33; 40

II. Health Hazards of a High Sugar Diet
  1. Obesity
    stored, fat
  2. Tooth Decay
    70; 600
  3. Heart Disease
    twice, sugar; fat, sugar
  5. Infection: Susceptibility to Disease
    five, six
  6. Irritability
    vitamin B, irritability

Substitution
  Carob cake
  Carob chip or applesauce cookies
  Whole wheat blueberry or raisin bagels
  Fruit juices
  Dried fruits
  Fruit pies
  Homemade soy ice cream or fruit sherbets

Substances Used As Sweeteners

Food Sweeteners	% Sweetness	Sweetness Compared to Sugar	Undesirable Effects
Sugars:			
Sucrose (regular table sugar	100	1	Obesity
Lactose (milk sugar)	15	1/7	Diabetes
Glucose	75	3/4	Dental cavities
Honey Fructose	125	1 1/4	Hypoglycemia
			Coronary heart disease (by increasing cholesterol)
Chemical Sweeteners:			
Saccharin	35,000	300	Lower blood sugar
Dulcin	25,000	250	Bitter aftertaste destroyed by cooking
Cyclamates	3,000	30	Toxic
New chemical: Aspartylphenyl-alanine	16,000	160	Toxic

Life and Health Magazine.

RECIPES

Session 1

Homemade Breadmaking
Made Easy

NOTES

100% WHOLE WHEAT BREAD

2 packages active dry yeast
1/4 cup warm water
2 1/2 cups hot water
1/4 to 1/2 cup honey
1 T. salt
1/4 cup oil
1 cup wheat germ
7 cups whole wheat flour

SOFTEN active dry yeast in 1/4 cup warm water.
COMBINE hot water, honey, salt, and oil in another bowl.
STIR in wheat germ.
ADD 4 cups whole wheat flour to make a moderately stiff dough.
ADD softened yeast mixture to dough.

ADD remaining flour.
TURN OUT on a lightly floured surface.
KNEAD until smooth and satiny.
SHAPE dough into a ball.
PLACE in lightly greased bowl.
COVER and let rise in a warm place until double (about 1 1/2 hours).
PUNCH down.
CUT into 2 portions (about 1 1/4 to 1 1/2 lbs. each).
SHAPE each into smooth ball.
SHAPE into loaves.
LET RISE until double (about 1 hour).
BAKE 30-35 minutes at 350 degrees F.

WHOLE WHEAT BREAD

2 packages active dry yeast
1/4 cup warm water
2 1/2 cups hot water
1/2 cup brown sugar
1 T. salt
1/4 cup oil
4 cups whole wheat flour
1 cup wheat germ
3 cups unbleached white flour

SOFTEN yeast in 1/4 cup warm water.
COMBINE hot water, sugar, salt, and oil in another bowl.
COOL to lukewarm.
STIR in whole wheat flour and wheat germ.
STIR in yeast.

ADD remaining flour to make moderately stiff dough.
TURN OUT on a lightly floured surface.
KNEAD until smooth and satiny.
SHAPE dough into a ball.
PLACE in lightly greased bowl.
COVER and let rise in a warm place until double (about 1 1/2 hours).
PUNCH down.
DIVIDE into 2 portions. (For smaller loaves, divide into 3 portions.)
SHAPE each into smooth ball.
SHAPE into loaves.
LET RISE until double (about 1 hour).
BAKE about 35 minutes at 350 degrees F.

NOTE: These bread recipes are designed to make either 2 or 3 loaves, depending on the size of the bread pan. For smaller loaves (1 1/4 to 1 1/2 lbs.) use pans approximately 3 x 7 x 2 1/4 in. deep. For larger loaves (1 3/4 to 2 lbs.) use 4 1/2 x 8 1/2 x 2 1/2 in. deep. Shape the loaf according to the size of the pan. The loaf will double in size when raised.

DANISH SWEET ROLLS

2 packages active dry yeast
1/4 cup warm water
2 1/2 cups water
1/2 cup brown sugar
1 T. salt
1/4 cup oil
1 cup oatmeal
1/2 cup wheat germ
3 cups whole wheat flour
4 cups unbleached white flour

SOFTEN active yeast in 1/4 cup warm
 water.
MIX ingredients together. (Follow same
 instructions as Whole Wheat Bread for
 making bread dough.)
LET rise.

PUNCH down after first rising of about
 1 1/2 hours.
ROLL OUT in 3 sections.
BRUSH dough with 2 T. melted butter.
SPRINKLE on 2 T. brown sugar.
COMBINE 1/3 cup raisins and nuts.
SPREAD on dough.
ROLL as for jelly roll.
SHAPE in ring.
PLACE on baking dish.
CUT almost to center.
COVER and let rise about 50 minutes.
BAKE at 350 degrees F. for about
 20-25 minutes.

OATMEAL RAISIN BREAD

2 T. active dry yeast
1/4 cup warm water
2 1/2 cups water
1/2 cup brown sugar
1 T. salt
1/4 cup oil
2 1/2 cups oatmeal
1 1/4 cups raisins
3 cups whole wheat flour
3 to 3 1/2 cups white flour

SOFTEN active yeast in 1/4 cup warm
 water.
COMBINE hot water, sugar, salt, and oil.
COOL to lukewarm.
STIR in oatmeal, raisins, and whole wheat
 flour.
STIR in yeast.
ADD remaining flour to make a moderately
 stiff dough.

TURN OUT on a lightly floured surface.
KNEAD until smooth and satiny.
SHAPE dough into a ball.
PLACE in lightly greased bowl.
COVER and let rise in warm place until
 double (about 1 1/2 hours).
PUNCH down.
CUT into 2 portions. (For smaller loaves,
 cut into 3 portions.)
SHAPE each into a smooth ball.
SHAPE into loaves.
LET RISE until double (about 1 hour).
BAKE about 30-35 minutes at 350
 degrees F.

RYE BREAD

```
2 packages active dry yeast
1/2 cup warm water
1 1/2 cups hot water
1/4 cup medium brown sugar
1/4 cup light molasses
1 T. salt
2 T. oil
2 1/2 cups medium rye flour
3 T. caraway seeds
1 cup whole wheat flour
2 1/2 to 3 cups unbleached
    white flour
```

SOFTEN active yeast in 1/2 cup warm water.
COMBINE hot water, sugar, salt, and oil.
COOL to lukewarm.

STIR in caraway seeds, rye flour, and whole wheat flour.
STIR in yeast.
ADD remaining flour to make a moderately stiff dough.
TURN OUT on a lightly floured surface.
KNEAD until smooth and satiny.
SHAPE dough into a ball.
PLACE in lightly greased bowl.
COVER and let rise in warm place until double (about 1 1/2 hours).
PUNCH down.
CUT into 2 portions.
SHAPE each into a smooth ball.
SHAPE into loaves.
LET RISE until double (about 1 hour).
BAKE about 35 minutes at 350 degrees F.

HEALTH BREAD

```
2 packages active dry yeast
1/2 cup warm water
2 3/4 cups boiling water
3/4 cup molasses
1 T. salt
2 T. oil
1 cup raisins
1 cup wheat germ
1 cup quick-cooking oats
1 cup bran
3 cups whole wheat flour
4 3/4 to 5 cups sifted unbleached
    white flour
```

SOFTEN yeast in warm water.
COMBINE boiling water, molasses, salt, oil, raisins, wheat germ, oats, and bran.
COOL.
ADD softened yeast.

STIR in whole wheat flour and 2 cups white flour.
ADD gradually enough flour to make a soft dough.
KNEAD until smooth.
PLACE in a greased bowl.
COVER and let rise in warm place until double (about 1 hour).
PUNCH down.
DIVIDE in half.
SHAPE into loaves.
PLACE in greased loaf pans.
LET RISE about 1 hour.
BAKE about 35-40 minutes at 350 degrees F.

OATMEAL PECAN BREAD

2 T. active dry yeast
1/4 cup warm water
2 1/2 cups water
1/2 cup brown sugar
1 T. salt
1/4 cup oil
1 cup oatmeal
1/2 cup pecan pieces
4 cups whole wheat flour
3 cups unbleached white flour

SOFTEN active yeast in 1/4 cup warm water.
COMBINE hot water, sugar, salt, and oil.
COOL to lukewarm.
STIR in oatmeal, pecan pieces, and whole wheat flour.

STIR in yeast.
ADD remaining flour to make a moderately stiff dough.
TURN OUT on a lightly floured surface.
KNEAD until smooth and satiny.
SHAPE dough into a ball.
PLACE in lightly greased bowl.
COVER and let rise in warm place until double (about 1 1/2 hours).
PUNCH down.
CUT into 2 portions. (For smaller loaves, cut into 3 portions.)
SHAPE each into a smooth ball.
SHAPE into loaves.
LET RISE until double (about 1 hour).
BAKE about 35 minutes at 350 degrees F.

APRICOT BREAD

1/2 cup warm water
3 T. yeast
3 cups hot water
3 T. raw or brown sugar
3 T. molasses
1 T. salt
3 T. oil
1 cup chopped dried apricots
1 cup oatmeal
1/2 cup bran
1/2 cup soy flour
4 cups stoneground whole wheat flour
1 1/2 - 2 cups whole wheat or
    white flour

SOFTEN active yeast in 1/2 cup warm water (in a separate bowl).
COMBINE hot water, sugar, salt, and oil.
STIR in dried apricots, oatmeal, bran, and soya flour.

ADD stoneground whole wheat flour to make a stiff dough.
STIR in yeast mixture.
ADD remaining whole wheat or white flour to mixture to make a moderately stiff dough.
TURN OUT on a lightly floured surface.
KNEAD until smooth and satiny.
DIVIDE in half.
SHAPE dough into a ball.
PLACE in lightly greased bowl.
COVER and let rise in warm place until double (about 1 1/2 hours).
PUNCH down.
CUT into 2 portions. (For smaller loaves, divide into 3 portions.)
SHAPE each one into a smooth ball.
SHAPE into loaves.
LET RISE until double (almost 1 hour).
BAKE about 45-50 minutes at 350 degrees F. or 180 degrees C.

HERB BREAD

```
    1/4 cup warm water
    3 T. yeast
    2 1/2 cups water
    3 T. milk powder (soy)
    3 T. honey or brown sugar
    3 T. oil
    1 T. salt
    1 t. thyme
    1 t. parsley
    1 t. sweet basil
    1 t. oregano
    1 t. marjoram
    8 cups 100% whole wheat flour
```

SOFTEN active yeast in 1/4 cup warm water.

COMBINE water, milk powder, honey, oil, salt, and seasonings in large bowl.

STIR until all is mixed in and dissolved.

STIR in yeast mixture.

ADD flour gradually to make a moderately stiff dough.

TURN OUT on a lightly floured surface.

KNEAD until smooth and satiny, adding four as necessary.

SHAPE dough into a ball.

PLACE in lightly greased bowl.

COVER and let rise in warm place until double (about 1 1/2 hours).

PUNCH down.

CUT into 2 portions. (For smaller loaves, cut into 3 portions.)

SHAPE each into a smooth ball.

SHAPE into loaves.

LET RISE until double (about 1 hour).

BAKE about 40 minutes at 350 degrees F.

PUMPERNICKEL BREAD

```
    3 packages active dry yeast or
        3 T. fresh yeast
    1 1/2 cups water
    1/2 cup dark molasses
    1 T. salt
    2 T. oil
    2 T. caraway seeds
    2 1/2 cups rye flour
    2 1/2 cups unbleached white flour
```

SOFTEN active yeast in warm water.

COMBINE 1 1/2 cups water with molasses, salt, oil and caraway seeds.

STIR in yeast mixture.

ADD flour to make a moderately stiff dough.

TURN OUT on a lightly floured surface.

KNEAD until smooth and satiny.

SHAPE dough into a ball.

PLACE in lightly greased bowl.

COVER and let rise in warm place until double (about 1 1/2 hours).

PUNCH down.

CUT into 2 portions.

SHAPE each into a smooth ball. (For round bread, place on opposite corners of a baking sheet.)

LET RISE until double (about 1 hour).

BAKE about 30 to 35 minutes at 350 degrees F.

DINNER OATMEAL ROLLS

1/2 cup warm water
3 T. yeast
4 cups boiling water
2 cups oatmeal
3/4 cup brown sugar
1 T. salt
1/3 cup oil
1 1/2 cups wheat germ
1 1/2 cups soy flour
4 cups stoneground whole wheat flour
3 cups unbleached white flour or
    whole wheat flour

SOFTEN yeast in 1/2 cup warm water.
POUR boiling water over oats.
ADD brown sugar, salt, and oil.
STIR in wheat germ, soy flour, and
    whole wheat flour.

STIR in yeast mixture.
ADD white flour gradually to make
    moderately stiff dough.
TURN OUT on a lightly floured surface.
KNEAD until smooth and satiny.
SHAPE dough into a ball.
PLACE in lightly greased bowl.
COVER and let rise in warm place until
    double (about 1 1/2 hours).
PUNCH down.
SHAPE into rolls.
LET RISE until double (about 35 to 40
    minutes).
BAKE 25 to 35 minutes at 350 degrees F.
    or 180 degrees C.

Makes approximately 2 dozen rolls.

POTATO ROLLS

2 T. dry active yeast or cake yeast
1/2 cup warm water
2 cups hot water
2 cups mashed potatoes
3 T. honey
1 T. salt
2 T. oil
1/2 cup wheat germ
1/4 cup soy flour
1 cup whole wheat flour
3 T. gluten flour (optional)
4 cups (approximately) "enriched"
    unbleached white flour

SOFTEN active yeast in 1/2 cup warm
    water.
COMBINE hot water, mashed potatoes,
    honey, salt, and oil.
COOL to lukewarm.

ADD wheat germ, soy flour, whole
    wheat and gluten flour.
STIR in yeast.
ADD remaining flour to make a moderately
    stiff dough.
TURN OUT on a lightly floured surface.
KNEAD until smooth and satiny.
SHAPE dough into a ball.
PLACE in lightly greased bowl.
COVER and let rise in warm place until
    double (about 1 1/2 hours).
SHAPE into rolls.
LET RISE about 40 minutes.
BAKE about 25 to 35 minutes at 350
degrees F.

HONEY BRAN ROLLS

> 1/2 cup oil
> 1 cup boiling water
> 1 cup bran
> 2/3 cup honey
> 1 1/2 t. salt
> 1 cup lukewarm water
> 1 package yeast
> 2 cups whole wheat flour
> 2 to 3 cups unbleached white.flour

COMBINE oil, boiling water, bran, honey, and salt.
STIR to blend.
COOL to lukewarm.
ADD yeast which has been softened in lukewarm water.
ADD flour gradually to make soft dough.
KNEAD until smooth and satiny.
LET RISE to double in bulk (1 1/2 hours).
GREASE HANDS well (dough is very sticky).
FORM into rolls.
DROP from spoon if using muffin tins.
LET RISE 35 to 40 minutes.
BAKE at 375 degrees F. for 25 to 40 minutes.

APPLESAUCE BREAD

> 2 T. yeast
> 1 cup water
> 1 T. molasses
> 2 cups warm applesauce
> 2 T. honey or brown sugar
> 1 t. salt
> 2 T. oil
> 1/2 cup wheat germ
> 1/2 cup soy flour
> 1 cup whole wheat flour
> 3 to 4 cups unbleached white flour

SOFTEN yeast in warm water.
ADD molasses to this mixture.
COMBINE applesauce, honey, salt, and oil.
ADD yeast mixture.
ADD wheat germ and flour to make dough.
KNEAD until smooth and satiny.
LET RISE to double in bulk (1 1/2 hours).
PUNCH down.
DIVIDE into 2 portions.
SHAPE into loaves.
LET RISE to double (about 1 hour).
BAKE at 350 degrees F. for 30 to 35 minutes.

RECIPES

Session 2

Making Breakfast
a Better Meal

NOTES

Scrambled Egg Tofu
1 box firm tofu   mash tofu
1 tbsp soy sauce   Add seasoning, soy sauce
1 tsp chicken seasoning   + turmeric
pinch turmeric   cook in skillet w/ little olive oil

BAKED OATMEAL

4 cups water
1 t. salt
3 cups oats
1/2 cup coconut
1/4 cup chopped dates
2 T. oil (optional)

BOIL water and salt.
MIX remaining ingredients.
ADD water all at once.
BAKE in shallow dish at 375 degees F. or 190 degrees C. for 30-40 minutes.

GRANOLA

7 cups oatmeal
1 cup wheat germ
1 cup coconut (finely ground)
1 1/2 t. salt
1 cup slivered almonds or chopped pecans, etc.
1/4 to 1/2 cup oil
1/2 cup warm water
1/4 to 1/2 cup honey
1 t. vanilla

MIX above dry ingredients together in large pan.
ADD liquid to dry ingredients.
MIX thoroughly.
PUT in large shallow pans.
BAKE at 225 degrees F. until golden brown and crisp (about 2 to 2 1/2 hours) or bake slowly at 170 degrees F. for 6-7 hours.
SERVE with fruit, if desired. Fresh peaches, strawberries, or fruit puree are especially delicious.

BREAKFAST BEANS — COUNTRY STYLE

1 lb. Great Northern beans
1 1/2 t. salt
2 T. oil (optional)
1 medium onion, chopped

WASH beans, looking over carefully.
ADD 6 cups water.
BRING to boil.
LET BOIL about 2 minutes.
SET OFF the heat.
LET STAND, covered, for 1 hour.
ADD onion and oil.

BRING to the boil and continue cooking on simmer heat until nearly done.
ADD the salt and finish cooking.
ADD enough water to make a "soupy" consistency.
SIMMER until beans are very tender.
SERVE over whole wheat toast.

SOY OAT WAFFLES

2 1/2 cups water
1 1/2 cups rolled oats
1 T. oil
1 cup soaked soybeans (= 1/2 cup
    dry soybeans)
1/2 t. salt

SOAK soybeans several hours in sufficient
    water to keep covered.
DRAIN.
COMBINE all ingredients.
BLEND until light and foamy.
BAKE in pre-heated hot waffle iron for
    8 minutes or until steam stops.

Due to the fact that there is no leavening in
these waffles, use a regular waffle iron —
not a Belgian waffle iron.

CASHEW OAT WAFFLES

3 cups water
3/4 cup cashews
1 cup soy milk powder
1/2 t. salt
1 T. brown sugar
1 t. vanilla
1 T. wheat germ
3 to 4 T. oil
2 1/2 cups oats

BLEND cashews in water until smooth and
    silky.
ADD other ingredients.
BLEND together.
LET STAND for 10 minutes to thicken.
COOK in hot waffle iron until golden
    brown.
COOK approximately 10 minutes.

BLUEBERRY TOPPING

1 qt. canned blueberries
2 to 3 T. cornstarch in water
    OR
3 to 4 cups fresh blueberries
3 to 4 cups apple or pineapple juice
2 to 3 T. cornstarch, tapioca, or
    arrowroot powder

COMBINE ingredients.
HEAT to the boil.
STIR in cornstarch, tapioca, or arrowroot
    powder to thicken.
SWEETEN to taste.

You may use other fruits to make this
topping such as peaches, or fruit cocktail in
its own juice.

SOY CREAM

1 cup soy milk
2 T. powdered vegetarian jello
    (Example: Emes Kosher-Jel)
1/4 cup cooked rice
1/4 cup oil
1 T. vanilla
1/2 cup strawberries*

BLEND soy milk, powdered vegetarian jello, and rice.
ADD vanilla.
BLEND oil in slowly.

*For strawberry cream, add fresh or frozen strawberries.

TROPICAL DRESSING

1 cup soy cream
1/2 cup crushed pineapple
1/4 cup coconut

MIX thoroughly.
SERVE with fruit salad.

APRICOT JAM

2 cups dried apricots
Unsweetened pineapple juice

SOAK dried apricots in unsweetened pineapple juice until soft.
ADD enough juice to cover apricots.
BLEND into a jam.

DOUGHNUTS

1 1/3 cups warm water
1 T. yeast
3 T. honey
1 t. salt
1/4 cup oil
1 1/2 cups whole wheat flour
2 1/2 cups unbleached white flour

CUT with a doughnut cutter.
PLACE on oiled cookie sheet.
LET RISE only enough to look like doughnuts.
BAKE at 350 degrees F. for 15-20 minutes.

DISSOLVE yeast in warm water.
ADD honey, salt, and oil.
ADD flour to liquid ingredients.
MIX flour only enough to get it wet. Over
    mixing will make doughnuts like rolls.
ROLL out approximately 1/3" thick.

APPLESAUCE TOAST DELIGHT

Whole Wheat Bread
Peanut butter
Applesauce

TOAST bread until golden brown.
SPREAD with creamy peanut butter.

HEAT applesauce until warm.
SERVE over the toast.

Sliced bananas on top will complete the morning delight.

CRISPY OAT CAKES

1 cup water
1/3 cup oil
1 t. salt
1 T. honey
4 cups oatmeal
1/2 cup whole wheat flour

EMULSIFY water and oil by beating well.
ADD and MIX the next ingredients.
PLACE by spoonfuls on cookie sheet.
FLATTEN with a fork.
BAKE at 350 degrees F. or 180 degrees C.
    for about 15 minutes.
TURN and BAKE on other side for
    approximately 5-10 minutes.

APPLESAUCE OAT CAKES

1/2 cup water
1/2 cup applesauce
1 t. salt
1 T. honey
1/2 cup wheat germ
1/4 cup whole wheat flour
3 cups oatmeal

EMULSIFY water and applesauce by
    beating well.
ADD and MIX the next ingredients.
PLACE by spoonfuls on cookie sheet.
FLATTEN with a fork.
BAKE at 350 degrees F. or 180 degrees C.
    for about 15 minutes.
TURN and BAKE on other side for
    approximately 5-10 minutes.

FRUIT SOUP

1 cup dried apricots — cut
1 cup pears — cut
1 cup apples — cut
1 cup raisins
Lemon juice from 1/2 fresh lemon
1 1/2 qt. water

BRING to boil.
SIMMER 45 minutes to 1 hour.
ADD 3 T. tapioca.
SIMMER until thick.

RICE AND FRUIT

2 cups cold cooked brown rice
1 pint strawberries
2 cups chopped fruit (peaches, pears, mangoes, or fruit cocktail in natural juice)
2 bananas
1/2 cup coarsely chopped nuts (optional)
1 cup soy cream

MIX ingredients.
CHILL.
GARNISH with any kind of fruit or berries, fresh or frozen.

BERRY COBBLER

1 package active dry yeast
1/4 cup water
2/3 cup soy milk, scalded
1/4 cup oil
1/3 cup brown sugar
1/2 t. salt
2 1/4 cups flour (whole wheat or half whole wheat, half white)
2 ripe bananas
1 16 oz. bag frozen black berries

SOFTEN active dry yeast in warm water.
COMBINE scalded milk, oil, sugar, and salt.

STIR in 1 cup of the flour.
ADD softened yeast and bananas.
BEAT well.
ADD the remaining flour.
BEAT thoroughly.
COVER and let rise in a warm place until almost double (1 hour).
PLACE in an oiled pan.
BRUSH top with a little oil.
ARRANGE berries over batter.
LET RISE until light (about 30 minutes).
BAKE in a moderate oven at 350 degrees F. or 180 degrees C. for 30-35 minutes.

APPLE PRUNE PUDDING

25-30 prunes
1 apple
1 T. lemon juice
sugar (to taste — optional)
4 T. potato flour
4 T. water

ADD peeled, cut apple.
COOK 20 minutes.
ADD lemon juice.
ADD sugar to taste (optional).
MIX potato flour with water.
ADD to prune pudding.

SOAK prunes 2 hours in 5 cups of water.
COOK 20 minutes.

APPLE CRISP

6 to 8 large apples, peeled and sliced
2 cups unsweetened pineapple juice
2-3 T. cornstarch

2 cups quick oats
1 cup whole wheat flour
1/4 cup wheat germ
1/4 cup nuts
1/4 cup brown sugar
1/4 t. salt
1 t. vanilla
1/2 cup oil
1/4 cup water

PLACE peeled and sliced apples in bottom of Pyrex baking dish.
THICKEN unsweetened pineapple juice with cornstarch. Whip to a smooth consistency.
POUR this mixture over apples.
MIX remaining ingredients thoroughly in a bowl.
SPREAD over sliced apples in shallow pan.
BAKE until golden brown in moderate oven (350 degrees F.) approximately 30 - 40 minutes.

Variations: Use this crumb topping on other fresh fruit and berries, or on thickened peaches or other canned fruit.

FRUIT TOAST

1 qt. fruit — berries, peaches, cherries
Sweeten to taste
Pinch of salt

HEAT to boiling.
MIX 2 T. cornstarch in 1/4 cup water.
ADD to hot fruit mixture.
STIR until thickened and clear.
SERVE on whole wheat toast or zwieback.

CREAMY COCONUT FRUIT SALAD

1 cup orange slices, cubed
1 cup pineapple
2 bananas, sliced
1 cup green grapes
1 cup shredded coconut
3/4 cup cream or tropical dressing

CHILL all ingredients.
PLACE together in a bowl.
ADD shredded coconut and cream last.
COMBINE gently.
CHILL thoroughly.

FRESH FRUIT SALAD

Peaches (several)
1 cantaloupe
1 cup watermelon balls
1 cup blueberries
1/2 can orange juice concentrate

PEEL and SLICE peaches.
PEEL and SLICE cantaloupe.
ADD watermelon balls and blueberries.
MIX in orange juice concentrate.
SERVE.

LAYERED APPLESAUCE

> 1/4 cup margarine
> 3 cups uncooked quick rolled oats
> 2 T. brown sugar
> 1/2 cup nuts, chopped
> applesauce

MELT butter in skillet on medium heat.
ADD rolled oats.
TOAST oats over medium heat.

STIR constantly until golden brown.
STIR in brown sugar.
ADD chopped nuts.
SERVE by placing 2 heaping T. of oat
    mixture in each bowl.
ADD the applesauce on top and finish with
    another layer of oat mixture.

Can be served with a little cream dribbled
over the top also. Makes about 6 servings.

RICE

> 3/4 cup brown or pudding rice
> 2 1/4 cups water
>
> 3 cups milk
> 1 t. salt
> 2 t. sugar (optional)

COOK rice in water for 10 minutes.
ADD milk, salt, and sugar.
SIMMER for 45 minutes.
WHIP soy cream with vanilla into rice.

UNLEAVENED GEMS

> 1 1/4 cup whole wheat flour
> 1 1/4 cup white flour
> 1/2 t. salt
> 1 cup water
> 1/3 cup oil

SIFT flour into bowl with salt.
ADD oil slowly while mixing.

ADD water and MIX well until smooth.
ADD a **little** more flour if sticky.
SHAPE biscuits **small** and quite **flat**.
BAKE at 375 degrees F. for 10 minutes,
    then reduce heat to 275 degrees for
    30 minutes or until baked through.

Can be broken into bowl with "Chicken"
Gravy poured over them.

"CHICKEN" GRAVY

> 1/3 cup oil
> 1/2 cup white flour
> 3-4 cups water
> 1 t. soy sauce
> 1 1/2 T. chicken seasoning

COOK until thick.
STIR constantly.
ADD chicken seasoning.

Note: For thicker gravy, use 3 cups water.
Gravy may be used over Unleavened Gems.

MIX oil and flour until smooth.
ADD water and soy sauce.

RECIPES

Session 3

Planning a
Balanced Menu

NOTES

BASIC FOOD GROUPS & MENU PLANNING GUIDE

1. a. Fruits: Two or more servings, of which one should be a citrus fruit or tomato daily.

   b. Vegetables: Two or more servings of vegetables other than potato, one of which should be of the deep green or yellow kind and one should be served raw.

2. Whole Grains: Two or more servings a day. At least one serving of a cereal or bread in some form.

3. Protein Foods: One or more servings daily.

4. Milk or milk alternate: Drink or combine with other foods.

CASHEW NUT LOAF

1 cup onion, chopped
1 1/2 cups celery, chopped
2 cans mushroom soup
2 cans water
2 envelopes George Washington Broth*
1 1/2 cups cashews
2 cans (5 oz.) Chinese noodles

MIX all ingredients together.
PLACE in casserole dish.
BAKE at 350 degrees F. for about 1 hour.

*Buy in health food store or substitute a seasoning broth.

CHOW MEIN

2 T. oil
2 cups peeled onion, sliced
1 cup sliced gluten

2 cups celery, sliced
1 green pepper, sliced
1 can water chestnuts, drained, sliced or 1/2 cup raw cashew nuts
1 can bean sprouts, drained
1 or 2 T. soy sauce or Bragg Liquid Aminos*
1 cup water
2 T. cornstarch

SAUTE onions, and gluten in oil.
ADD and COOK remaining ingredients quickly, stirring constantly.
THICKEN with cornstarch mixed with a little water.
SERVE over rice.

*Buy in health food store. This is an unfermented soy sauce with no added salt.

ITALIAN SAUCE (for pizza)

1 onion, chopped
1/4 cup oil
2 qts. tomatoes (blended)
4 large cans tomato paste
1 t. salt
1 T. Italian seasoning
1 bay leaf
Pinch of garlic salt (or one clove of fresh garlic cut up)

SAUTE onion in oil.
ADD blended tomatoes, tomato paste, and remaining ingredients.
SIMMER for about 3 hours or until sauce becomes thick.

For pizza dough, use basic bread recipe.

BROCCOLI WITH RICE

1 cup brown rice (cooked)
1 bunch fresh broccoli spears (or frozen)
1 can mushroom soup
1/2 cup soy mayonnaise
1 t. McKay's chicken seasoning*
1 t. tumeric
1/4 cup slivered almonds

ARRANGE on top of rice.
COMBINE mushroom soup, soy mayonnaise, and seasonings. (For thinner sauce, add 1 cup milk.)
TOP rice with sauce mixture.
SPRINKLE almonds on top.
BAKE 20 minutes at 350 degrees F. or until bubbly.
SERVE immediately.

COOL brown rice.
SPREAD in flat casserole dish.
PARBOIL broccoli.

*Buy in health food store or substitute a seasoning broth.

GREEN BEANS IN TOMATO SAUCE

1 qt. canned green beans, drained
1 qt. canned tomatoes, blended
1 4-oz. can tomato paste
1/2 t. Italian seasoning
1/2 t. oregano
1/4 t. onion salt
1/4 t. garlic salt

ADD drained green beans to rest of the ingredients.
COOK until sauce is cooked up into green beans.

61

SOY MAYONNAISE

3/4 cup water
1/2 cup Soyagen* or other soy milk
    powder
1 package George Washington
    Broth*
1/4 t. onion salt
1/4 t. garlic powder
3/4 cup oil
2 lemons, juiced or 4 T. Realemon

BLEND water, soy milk powder, broth,
    salt and garlic powder.
GRADUALLY ADD oil in blender.
STIR in lemon juice.

*Buy in health food store or substitute
appropriately.

For successful mayonnaise, the oil must be
added **slowly** or **dribbled** in. Be sure to
stir in the lemon juice. Do not blend it in.

TARTAR SAUCE

1 cup soy mayonnaise
2 T. chopped homemade dill pickle
2 T. onion, finely chopped
2 T. pimiento
2 T. green pepper, finely chopped
2 T. lemon juice
1/2 t. paprika
salt to taste

MIX all ingredients together lightly.
USE with entree or as a dip for raw or
    cooked vegetables.

BEET SALAD

1 can diced beet
1 small onion, diced
Soy Mayonnaise to taste
salt to taste

MIX all ingredients together.

Green beans may be added for variety.

CABBAGE SALAD

1 cabbage, chopped
1 can unsweetened crushed
    pineapple
1/2 cup nuts
Soy Mayonnaise
salt to taste

MIX all ingredients together.

CRACKERS

3 cups quick oats, uncooked
2 cups unbleached flour
1 cup wheat germ
3 T. sugar (optional)
1/2 t. salt
3/4 cup oil
1 cup water

MIX all ingredients together.
ROLL out on two large cookie sheets to the edge or turn sheets over and use pan without edges. Roll dough thin.
SPRINKLE with salt.
CUT into desired shape.
BAKE at 325 degrees F. for about 30 minutes.

VEGETABLE POT PIE

2 cups potatoes, diced small
1 1/2 cups carrots, diced small
1/2 small onion, chopped
1 16 oz. package frozen peas
1 cup gluten or textured vegetable protein (Worthington FriChik is great)

Cream Sauce:
2 T. flour
2 T. oil
2 cups soy milk
2 t. vegetable stock

STEAM potatoes, carrots, onion, until tender.
ADD vegetable protein and peas.
MIX lightly.
PLACE this mixture in casserole dish.

COMBINE Cream Sauce ingredients.
COOK together on low to medium heat, stirring constantly until thickened.
POUR over vegetables in casserole dish.
COVER with pie crust. (See page 78)
BAKE in hot oven, 425-450 degrees F. for 20 minutes or until nicely browned.

ONE MEAL VEGETABLE DISH

3 cups fresh green beans, cut
2 cups carrots, cut in rings
1 1/2 cups cauliflower, cut in small chunks
1/4 cup fresh green onion tops
1 cup water
1/4 cup whole shelled almonds
1/2 t. Vegex or vegetable broth
2 T. cornstarch with a little water to thicken (use only as needed)

SAUTE onion in a little oil.
ADD green beans and cook with onions and 1/2 of water for 5 minutes.
ADD carrots.
COOK for another 5 minutes.
ADD cauliflower.
COOK until vegetables are tender.
ADD almonds and seasonings and the cornstarch mixture.
SERVE when vegetables are still crisp.

EGGPLANT A LA CREOLE

1 large eggplant (aubergines)
2 T. vegetable oil
1 onion, chopped
1 clove garlic
1 green pepper, chopped
1 cup vegeburger or gluten (optional)
3 T. flour
1 t. salt
1 qt. tomatoes, blended
1 or 2 bay leaves
1/2 cup bread crumbs

PEEL and cut eggplant into thick slices.
    Cut again into 1" dices.
COOK in small amount of salted water
    until just tender.

DRAIN and PUT into oiled baking dish.
SAUTE onion and green pepper in oil.
BROWN vegeburger and ADD to onion
    and bell pepper mixture.
SPRINKLE flour and salt over this and
    STIR in.
ADD tomatoes and bay leaf.
STIR gently.
COOK for a few minutes over low heat.
REMOVE bay leaf.
POUR over eggplant.
COVER all with a layer of bread crumbs.
BAKE in moderate oven, 300 degrees F.
    for 20 to 30 minutes.

ITALIAN RICE-VEGETABLE SOUP

3 T. oil
3 T. uncooked brown rice
1 large onion, chopped
3 pints water (1 1/2 liters)
2 vegetable stock cubes (Knorr)
2-3 sticks of celery, chopped
1 large carrot or 2 small (cut into
    thin, short sticks)
1 14-oz. can of tomatoes, sliced
    (do not add juice)
1/2 green pepper (cut like carrots)
4 oz. mushrooms, sliced
salt to taste
thyme or Italian seasoning
4 oz. mixed corn and green peas
chopped parsley

SIMMER brown rice and onion in oil until
    onion is tender.
ADD water, vegetable stock cubes, celery
    and carrots.
SIMMER 25 minutes.
ADD tomatoes, green pepper, mushrooms,
    salt, and thyme or Italian seasoning.
SIMMER 5 minutes.
ADD corn and green peas.
SERVE with chopped parsley.

TABOULI (serves 6)

1 1/4 cups bulgar wheat 1 t. salt 1 1/2 cups boiling water DRESSING: 3 T. olive oil 3 T. lemon juice 1/2 t. oregano 1 to 2 T. fresh mint, finely chopped 1 clove garlic, finely chopped 6 T. fresh parsley, finely chopped 3 green onions, finely sliced 1 large fresh tomato, chopped 1/2 cucumber, chopped 1/2 green pepper, chopped	MIX bulgar wheat and salt. POUR boiling water over mixture and leave for 20 minutes. MIX dressing ingredients together. POUR over bulgar wheat and MIX together. LEAVE overnight. ADD tomatoes, cucumbers, and green pepper. SERVE with brown pita bread.

RICE CROQUETTES

1 cup chopped pecans 1 cup cooked brown rice 1 cup whole wheat bread crumbs 1 T. soy flour 1 1/2 t. salt 1 T. chopped parsley 1 small onion (finely chopped) 1 cup soy milk	COMBINE all ingredients. SHAPE into croquettes. PLACE on oiled cookie sheet. BAKE in pre-heated oven at 350 degrees F. until golden brown, about 40 to 45 minutes. SERVE with gravy.

SPLIT PEA SOUP

2 1/4 cups green or yellow split peas 1 onion 1 cup diced celery 1 t. salt 1/4 t. marjoram 2 qts. water	COVER peas with water. BRING to the boil. REDUCE heat and ADD onion, celery, salt, and marjoram. SIMMER until peas are cooked to a soup consistency (about 2 hours).

THREE BEAN SALAD

1 can or 1 cup green beans (cooked)
1 can or 1 cup red kidney beans
  (cooked)
1 can or 1 cup garbanzos (cooked)
1/4 cup green pepper, finely diced
1/2 cup celery, diced
1/4 cup red pepper, diced
1 green onion, finely diced
1/4 cup lemon juice
2 T. oil
1/2 t. salt

COMBINE all ingredients.
ALLOW to sit in the refrigerator several
  hours before serving.

GLUTEN IN ONION, PEPPER TOMATO SAUCE

Gluten
2 to 3 T. oil
2 to 3 onions (cut in strips)
1 large green pepper (cut in strips)
1 large can tomatoes or 3 to 4 fresh
  tomatoes
3 T. tomato paste
onion salt to taste, about 1/2 t.
garlic salt to taste, about 1/2 t.
Italian seasoning to taste, about 1/2 t.
Sweet basil to taste, about 1/2 t.

SAUTE onion, green peppers.
ADD tomatoes and tomato paste.
ADD seasonings to taste.
BAKE gluten with gluten broth until
  crispy.
THEN ADD baked gluten to vegetable
  mixture.

SUNFLOWER SEED CASSEROLE

2 cups sunflower seeds
2 cups cashews
3/4 cup water
1 cup mushrooms
5 cups cooked brown rice
2 1/2 t. vegetable broth
salt, to taste
onion, finely chopped
3 T. soy sauce
2 T. Brewers yeast
1/8 t. garlic powder

GRIND sunflower seeds fine.
BLEND cashews and water in blender
  until smooth.
COMBINE all ingredients.
MIX thoroughly.
PUT in casserole dish.
BAKE 1 1/2 hours at 325 degrees F.
LEAVE cover on first 45 minutes.

POTATO SOUP

2 cups potatoes, diced
4 to 5 cups water
1 onion, diced
1 t. salt

1 packet vegetable bouillon
1 T. parsley
1/4 t. marjoram
1/4 t. thyme
1/4 t. sweet basil
1 cup milk

COOK potatoes and onion in salted water
    until tender.
MASH or blend potatoes.
ADD vegetable bouillon and remaining
    herbs.
ADD milk and SIMMER. Do not boil.

NUT LOAF

3 cups raw ground cashew nuts
2 cups vegeburger or ground gluten
2 medium onions, chopped
1/4 cup celery, chopped
3 T. oil (optional)
1 cup bread crumbs
1 cup milk
2 T. corn starch or egg replacer
3 t. McKay's chicken seasoning
1 T. soy sauce
1/2 t. salt

MIX all ingredients together.
POUR into oiled pan and COVER with foil.
SET in a shallow pan of water.
BAKE at 350 degrees F. for 1 hour.
UNCOVER and REMOVE from water for
    the last 10 minutes of baking.

CHICKEN ROAST

2 cups seasoned bread crumbs
2 cups water
1 cup onion, chopped
1 cup celery, chopped
3 T. oil (optional)
4 1/2 cups ground chicken soyameat
2 t. McKay's chicken seasoning
2 T. soy flour or egg replacer
1/2 t. salt
1 cup milk

SOAK bread crumbs in water.
SAUTE onions and celery in the oil and
    ADD to bread crumbs.
MIX in all remaining ingredients.
POUR into greased casserole dish.
BAKE 1 hour at 350 degrees F.

DRINKS

FRUIT PUNCH

5 cups unsweetened pineapple
  juice, chilled
1 qt. apple juice, chilled
1 package (10 oz.) frozen
  strawberries, partially thawed
1 qt. sparkling mineral water
Fresh strawberry slices
Fresh lime slices

COMBINE pineapple and apple juices
  in punch bowl.
BLEND strawberries, undrained, in
  blender.
MIX into pineapple/apple juice.
POUR in mineral water just before
  serving.
GARNISH with strawberry and lime slices.

ORANGE BANANA DRINK

3 cups unsweetened pineapple juice
3 large bananas
2 (12 oz.) cans frozen orange juice
1 (12 oz.) can frozen lemonade

BLEND bananas with pineapple juice.
MIX with orange juice and lemonade,
  adding the amount of water called
  for in frozen juices.

APPLE ORANGE PUNCH

2 cups apple juice
2 qts. pineapple orange juice
1 qt. lemonade
2 cups cranberry juice
ice cubes

COMBINE together.
ADD ice cubes.

RECIPES

Session 4

Adequate Protein Inexpensively: The Advantages of a Vegetarian Diet

GLUTEN AND GLUTEN BROTH

Gluten:
8 cups whole wheat flour
4 cups water

Broth:
2 qts. water
1 onion, diced
1 T. Vegex
1/2 t. garlic powder
1/3 c. soy sauce
2 T. oil (optional)

MIX flour and water.
KNEAD thoroughly.
COVER dough entirely with water.

LET SOAK for at least 1 hour.
WASH or rinse thoroughly, keeping the dough together.
CONTINUE working the dough in water until you have a tough elastic lump which is mainly gluten, the protein of the wheat.
SLICE gluten into steak-like pieces and add to boiling broth.
SIMMER until most of liquid is gone.

Remaining broth may be thickened into a gravy and served over gluten steaks. Gluten may be breaded and baked, or browned in skillet.

LENTIL STEW

1/2 cup celery, chopped
1 onion, chopped
1 cup carrots, sliced
2 cups potatoes, diced
1 cup dry lentils
1 t. salt
2 T. parsley
1 qt. water
1 can tomatoes (1 lb., 12 oz.), chopped
1/4 t. thyme

PLACE all ingredients (except tomatoes) in saucepan.
COOK on low heat for about 1 hour.
ADD tomatoes to cook last 15 minutes.

OATBURGERS

4 1/2 cups water
1/2 cup soy sauce
4 1/2 cups oats
1 onion, chopped
1 t. garlic powder
1/4 cup Brewers yeast
2 T. oil

2 tbsp gluten

BRING water, soy sauce, and seasoning to the boil.
TURN DOWN heat.
ADD onion and oats.
FORM into patties.
BAKE until nicely browned at 350 degrees F. for about 45 minutes.
TURN after 20 minutes.

BAKED LENTILS

2 cups lentils, dry
5 cups water
1 T. molasses (optional)
1 t. oil (optional)
1 onion, chopped
1 can tomatoes (1 lb., 12 oz.),
    blended
1 t. salt

COOK lentils in water.
ADD rest of ingredients when water is
    all cooked up.
PLACE in baking dish.
BAKE at 350 degrees F. for 1 hour or
    longer.

LENTIL ROAST

1 c. dry
lentils + 2
c. H₂O =
2 c. cooked
lentils

2 cups lentils, cooked
1 cup nuts (chopped walnuts,
    pecans, etc.)
2 cups soy milk
1 small onion, chopped
1 t. salt
1/2 t. sage
1/4 to 1/2 t. garlic powder
1 1/2 cups dry bread crumbs or
    cereal flakes (corn flakes)

MIX all ingredients.
BAKE at 350 degrees F. for about
    1 hour.

SOY-OAT PATTIES WITH TOMATO SAUCE

1 cup soaked soy beans
1/2 cup water
2 T. flake yeast or 1 T. powdered
    yeast
1 T. soy sauce
1 T. oil
1/4 t. onion powder
1/4 t. garlic powder
1 t. Italian seasoning
1/2 t. salt
2/3 cup oats

COMBINE all ingredients, except oats,
    in blender and chop.
PLACE in bowl.
ADD rolled oats.
LET STAND 10 minutes.
DROP from one-fourth cup scoop on to
    oiled baking pan.
FLATTEN patty with spatula.
BAKE at 350 degrees F. for 10 minutes.
TURN OVER.
BAKE 10 more minutes.

TOMATO SAUCE

1 onion, chopped
3 cans tomatoes (1 lb., 12 oz.),
    blended
3 jars tomato paste (10.6 oz.)
3 t. salt
3 T. Italian seasoning
1 t. garlic powder
3 bay leaves
1 T. sweet basil

COMBINE all ingredients together.
SIMMER for 2 hours.

SHAMBURGERS

2 cups dry burger in water to
    re-hydrate
1 8-oz. can mushroom soup
1 cup quick oats
2 T. flour
1 onion, chopped
2 t. celery salt
1/2 t. Lawry's Seasoned Salt
1/2 t. salt (optional)
1/2 t. garlic powder
1/2 to 1 cup bread crumbs

MIX all ingredients together.
FORM into patties.
SAUTE in a little oil until golden brown.
TURN over.
BROWN on the other side.

OATMEAL-MUSHROOM STEAKS

1 onion, chopped
3 T. margarine
1 can (4 oz.) mushrooms (stems
    and pieces)
2 cups uncooked oatmeal
1 t. Vegex in 1/2 cup HOT water
1/2 cup milk
1 t. Lawry's Seasoned Salt
1/2 t. thyme
1/2 t. poultry seasoning
1 can mushroom soup
2 cans hot water with 1/2 t. Vegex

SAUTE onions in margarine until clear.
COMBINE all ingredients except
    mushroom soup and 2 cans of hot
    water with Vegex.
MIX well.
LET mixture stand in a covered bowl for
    45 minutes.
MOLD into small patties.
FRY in hot oil until browned.
ARRANGE in baking dish.
COVER with mixture of mushroom soup,
    hot water, and VEGEX.
BAKE at 350 degrees F. for about 1 hour.

WHEAT GERM PATTIES

1 1/2 cups wheat germ
1 cup uncooked oatmeal
1/2 cup chopped nuts
4 t. soy sauce
1/2 t. salt
1/4 t. sage
1 clove garlic or 1 t. garlic powder
1 medium onion, minced
1 cup soy milk

MIX well.
FORM into patties.
BROWN both sides in oil.
PLACE in baking dish.
COVER with mushroom soup or tomato sauce.
BAKE at 350 degrees F. for 10 to 15 minutes.

PECAN PATTIES

1 cup pecan meal
1 cup cold water
1 t. soy sauce
1/2 t. onion salt
1/2 t. Accent
Pinch garlic salt
1 cup rolled oats

BLEND briefly.
PLACE in bowl.
COMBINE oats.
DROP on lightly oiled skillet.
COOK at medium temperature until nicely browned on both sides.
COVER while cooking.

BAKED BEANS

2 1/2 cups (1 lb.) dried beans
  (Great Northern or navy)
7 cups boiling water
2 cups tomatoes (blended)
2 t. salt
2 T. tomato paste
2 T. brown sugar
2 T. molasses
2 T. oil
1 large, whole onion

SORT and WASH beans.
ADD beans to boiling water.
BRING to a full boil.
TURN OFF heat.
LET STAND for an hour or more.
BRING to a boil and boil for 1 hour.*
ADD all other ingredients to beans.
PLACE in bean pot.
BAKE for 1 hour at 350 degrees F. or bake in slow oven for 2 hours at 275 to 300 degrees F.

Soy Beans—soak in H2O in refrigerator. Can freeze in ziploc.

*There is some evidence that beans cooked by this method cause less intestinal gas.

74

RECIPES

Session 5

Simple, Healthful Desserts

NOTES

DATE LAYER BARS

1/2 cups margarine
1/2 cup brown sugar
1 1/2 cups unbleached white flour
1 t. salt
1 1/2 cups quick-cooking
 rolled oats
1 T. wheat germ
1/2 cup nuts
1 T. water
1 recipe date filling (see below)

Filling:
2 cups pitted dates
2 cups water

CREAM together margarine and sugar.
STIR dry ingredients into creamed
 mixture.

ADD water and MIX until crumbly.
FIRMLY PAT one-half of the mixture into
 greased baking dish.
SPREAD with date filling.
TOP with remaining crumbs.
PAT smooth.
BAKE at 350 degrees F. for about 30
 minutes.

Date Filling:
COMBINE ingredients in saucepan.
COVER.
COOK, stirring often until consistency of
 jam.
ADD more water as needed.

CAROB CARAMELS

1 cup coconut
1/2 cup carob powder
1 cup soy milk powder
1/2 cup honey
1 t. vanilla
1/4 t. salt
2 T. margarine
nuts, finely chopped

COMBINE all ingredients, except nuts,
 together.
PRESS firmly and smoothly into pan.
SPRINKLE finely chopped nuts over the
 top.

DRIED FRUIT CANDY

2 cups dried apricots, ground
1 cup dates, ground
1 cup raisins, ground
1/2 cup nuts, crushed

MIX the above ingredients together.
FORM into small balls.
ROLL in 1/2 cup crushed nuts.

BANANA NUT CAKE

2 packages yeast
2/3 cup water
1/2 cup vegetable oil
1 1/2 cups honey
1/2 cup brown sugar
1 T. soy milk
2 t. salt
2 t. vanilla
3 mashed ripe bananas
1 cup chopped pecans
3 cups unbleached white flour

DISSOLVE yeast in water for 10 to 15 minutes.
MIX oil, honey, brown sugar, milk and salt together.
CREAM thoroughly, mixing with mixer for about 5 or 6 minutes.
ADD vanilla and bananas.
BEAT well.
ADD this to the yeast mixture.
ADD chopped nuts.
SIFT flour and ADD to creamed mixture.
PLACE mixture in 2 round cake pans.
LET RISE 1 1/2 hours in warm place.
BAKE at 300 degrees F. for 50 minutes.

COCONUT PECAN FROSTING

1 cup soy milk
1/4 cup brown sugar
4 t. corn flour
1 T. margarine
1 t. vanilla
1 cup coconut, shredded
1 cup pecans

COMBINE soy milk, brown sugar, corn flour, margarine, and vanilla.
COOK and stir over medium heat until mixture thickens.
ADD coconut and pecans.
SPREAD over cake.

CARROT PIE

1 cup dates
2 1/2 T. cornstarch
3/4 t. salt
3 T. soy flour
1 t. vanilla
3 T. oil
1 3/4 cup cooked carrots*
1 1/2 cup soy milk

WHIZ all ingredients in blender.
POUR into pie plate that has been lined with crust.
BAKE at 350 degrees F. until set, about 35 minutes.
TOP with Soy Cream or whipped cream topping.

*Pumpkin or squash may be used in place or carrots.

PIE CRUST (one 10" pie crust)

> 2 cups pastry flour or unbleached
>   white flour
> 1/4 cup wheat germ
> 1 t. salt
> 1/2 cup vegetable oil
> 1/2 cup boiling water

MIX salt and flour.
POUR water and oil in all at once.
STIR with a fork.

ROLL between two oiled papers (wax
     paper).
REMOVE top paper.
LAY crust side down on pie pan.
REMOVE top oil paper.
FLUTE edges. (Moisten fluted edges so
     crust will not shrink in oven. Prick
     pastry to prevent puffing while baking.)
BAKE at 425 degrees F. for 15 minutes
     for baked pie shell. Watch closely —
     do not overbake.

APPLESAUCE COOKIES

> 1/2 cup honey or brown sugar
> 1/2 cup oil
> 1 cup applesauce
> 1/2 cup chopped nuts
> 1/2 t. salt
> 1 t. vanilla
> 4 cups quick oats

BEAT oil and sugar together until well
     blended.
ADD remaining ingredients.
MIX well.
DROP from teaspoon onto oiled
     cookie sheet.
BAKE at 325 degrees F. for 20 to 25
     minutes, or until nicely browned.
LET COOL before removing from
     cookie sheet.

ICE CREAM

> 2 cups water
> 1 cup cashews
> 1/2 cup brown sugar
> 1 t. salt
> 2 T. vanilla
> 6 T. agar flakes or gelatin
> 2 cups soy milk
> 1 cup soyamel* powder
> 1/2 cup oil
> 2 cups strawberries

BLEND water, cashews, brown sugar,
     salt, vanilla, and agar flakes or gelatin.
ADD soy milk, soyamel powder, and oil
     and BLEND.
ADD strawberries and BLEND.
POUR into ice cream freezer.

*Buy at health food store.

CAROB-APPLE BROWNIES

3/4 cup brown sugar
1 cup shredded raw apple
3/4 cup oil
1/2 t. salt
1 t. vanilla
1/2 cup chopped walnuts
3/4 cup carob powder
2 cups rolled oats

COMBINE sugar, apple, and oil.
BEAT until well blended.
ADD remaining ingredients.
MIX.
LET STAND for 10 minutes for oats to absorb moisture.
TURN onto oiled pan (1 1/2" thick). Use approximate 8 x 8 dish.
BAKE at 350 degrees F. for 25 minutes.
CUT into squares when cool.

CASHEW-DATE BANANA PIE

20 pitted dates
2/3 cup cashews
2 cups water
1/2 t. salt
1 t. vanilla
1 large banana

WHIZ cashews, dates, and 1 cup water in blender.
ADD salt, vanilla, and 2nd cup of water.
COOK until thick.
SLICE half of large banana in bottom of baked crust.
POUR cooled filling into crust.
TOP with rest of banana.
MAY SERVE with whipped topping.

NUTRITIOUS APPLE PIE

6 or 7 tart apples
1 cup apple juice concentrate
1/8 t. salt
1/2 to 1 t. coriander
2 T. cornstarch flour or tapioca
2 T. water
1 T. margarine (optional)

PEEL and SLICE apples.
PLACE in saucepan.
SIMMER over medium heat in apple juice for 8 to 10 minutes.
ADD salt and coriander.
ADD cornstarch mixed with water.
POUR mixture into unbaked pie shell.
DOT with margarine (optional).
BAKE at 350 degrees F. for 45 to 50 minutes.

APPLE RICE PUDDING

1/2 cup dry brown rice
2 cups apple juice
1/4 t. salt
1 T. margarine (optional)
2 T. raisins
1 t. vanilla
1 cup diced apples
3 T. honey

COMBINE first 6 ingredients.
BRING to the boil.
COOK over low heat for approximately 45 minutes.
ADD apples and honey.
COOK 10 more minutes.

OLD-FASHIONED BREAD PUDDING

2 1/4 cups milk
2 cups cubed bread
1/2 t. coriander
1/4 to 1/2 cup brown sugar
1 t. vanilla
1/4 t. salt
1/2 cups seedless raisins
1/2 cup chopped, peeled apples

MIX together.
POUR mixture into 8-inch round baking dish.
PLACE in shallow pan with water around it.
BAKE at 350 degrees F. about 45 minutes.

SUMMER FRUIT SALAD

3 fresh peaches, sliced
1 medium cantaloupe, peeled and cubed
1 cup watermelon balls
1 cup fresh blueberries
1/2 of 6-oz. can of frozen orange juice concentrate

TOSS fruits together gently.
ADD orange juice concentrate, undiluted.
SERVE well chilled.

Variations: Use strawberries, raspberries, honeydew melon, or other fresh fruit in season. Or use a mixture of fresh and frozen fruits. Avoid fruits that have been preserved in a syrup heavy with sugar.

APPLE DUMPLINGS

4 medium golden delicious apples
whole, pitted dates
cinnamon (or orange rind)
Two-crust pastry

Glaze:
1 12-oz. can frozen apple juice
    concentrate
1 12-oz. can water
2 1/2 T. cornstarch

CUT each apple in half, peel, and core.
PLACE one date in hollowed-out area
    of each half apple.
SPRINKLE with cinnamon or orange rind.
ROLL out pie crust into rectangle.
CUT into eight pieces.

PLACE one apple half in corner of pastry
    piece and wrap around apple.
REPEAT process with each piece of apple.
PLACE on greased cookie sheet.
BAKE at 375 degrees F. for approximately
    35 minutes. (Check with fork to be
    sure apples are tender.)
DISSOLVE cornstarch in small amount of
    cold water.
MIX together with other glaze ingredients.
COOK over medium heat, stirring
    occasionally, until thickened.
POUR over apples.
BAKE 10 more minutes.
SERVE topped with whipped cream or
    your favorite topping and chopped nuts.

NATURAL APPLE PIE

6 cups apples, peeled and sliced
1 6-oz. can frozen apple juice
    concentrate, undiluted
2 T. cornstarch
Pinch of salt
Apple pie spice to taste
Margarine
Two-crust pastry

DISSOLVE cornstarch in half the apple
    juice concentrate.
COMBINE with cornstarch, salt, spice,
    and margarine.
SIMMER until thickened, stirring
    occasionally.
POUR into pastry-lined pan.
DOT with margarine.
COVER with top crust.
BAKE at 375 degrees F. for 45 minutes.